THE WORKING PHOTOGRAPHER:

The Complete Manual
For The Money-Making Professional

THE WORKING PHOTOGRAPHER:

The Complete Manual
For The Money-Making Professional

Marija & Tod Bryant

AVON
PUBLISHERS OF BARD, CAMELOT, DISCUS AND FLARE BOOKS

Grateful acknowledgment is made to the following for permission
to reprint:

Edith and Phillip Leonian, "Copyright and Practice of the
Trade," © Edith & Phillip Leonian 1979.

Quotes on pages 28 and 67, Henri Cartier-Bresson, *The Decisive
Moment,* copyright © 1952 by Henri Cartier-Bresson, Verve and
Simon & Schuster.

Quotes on pages 79 and 94 by Miguel de Cervantes and Aldous
Huxley from *The 365 Great Quotes-A-Year Calendar 1983* © 1982
Workman Publishing.

THE WORKING PHOTOGRAPHER: A COMPLETE
MANUAL FOR THE MONEY-MAKING PROFES-
SIONAL is an original publication of Avon Books. This
work has never before appeared in book form.

AVON BOOKS
A division of
The Hearst Corporation
1790 Broadway
New York, New York 10019

Copyright © 1985 by Marija Bryant and Tod Bryant
Published by arrangement with the authors
Library of Congress Catalog Card Number: 84-45574
ISBN: 0-380-89526-9

Library of Congress Cataloging in Publication Data

Bryant, Tod.
  The working photographer.

  1. Photography, Commercial. 2. Photography—
Business methods. I. Bryant, Marija. II. Title.
TR690.B76 1985   770'.68   84-45574
ISBN 0-380-89526-9

First Avon Printing, February, 1985

ACKNOWLEDGMENTS

Grateful thanks to all the people who took time to talk to us, sharing their knowledge and experience. In addition to those quoted in the book the following people and organizations provided invaluable information.

Photographers

Frank Maresca, Les Fincher, Mark Darley, Paul Margolies, Martin Benjamin, Bill Crofton, Gary Blumenstein, Steve Goldstrohm and Kim Davis, Valerie Santagto.

Art or Creative Directors and Account Execs

Ed Socher, Ted French, W. R. Burchelle, Hamilton Wilson, Beth King, Marti Spinks Nunn, Sonny Fireci, Debbie Caitz, Ben Sarao.

Schools and Professional Associations

The Portfolio Center of Atlanta, The Fishback School, The Art Institutes, New York Institute of Photography, Ohio Institute of Photography, ASMP, APA, SPAR PPofA.

In addition, there are people who don't fit into categories whom we'd like to thank for general, all-around encouragement. Bob Gonsor for believing in a couple of freelancers. Dick Ennis and Dick Kitchen for encouraging a high school kid with a photo habit. Brad Elliott for patience with fear of writing. Bill Alexander, our editor, for general tolerance and believing that we could do it. And Chris Miller for the patience to deal with first-time authors.

Mostly, we'd like to thank them for keeping their sense of humor.

*To our families
for their inspiration,
encouragement and—
most of all—love.*

THE WORKING PHOTOGRAPHER:

The Complete Manual
For The Money-Making Professional

CONTENTS

INTRODUCTION

The market for photography is tremendous. Next time you pass a newsstand, stop and leaf through a magazine—any magazine. See all those ads? Those illustrations for stories? Those portraits of celebrities? That's just a small part of a market that includes corporate photography, public relations, architectural, scientific, audiovisual, travel photography, portraits, and more.

The photographers who shoot these pictures all started out like you—with interest and skill and ambition. Through experience, trial and error, and—face it, it is important—luck, they now get paid to do what they enjoy.

That sounds like a wonderful way to make a living. And it is. But starting out is about as wonderful as trying to sell encyclopedias door-to-door. (In fact, you sometimes suspect an encyclopedia salesman gets a more enthusiastic welcome than a starting-out photographer.)

We wrote this book to make that beginning period as painless as possible. This book tells you how to find the photo jobs and the people who assign them, how to prepare yourself to get the job, how to do the job right once you get it, and how to keep the jobs coming. Along with the facts, we've included some "street smarts": tricks of the trade that we've picked up over the last ten years, techniques that have worked for other photographers, and pointers from art directors and other buyers of photography.

We talked to photographers and to buyers of photography in different parts of the country and in a wide variety of specialties—freelancers, staffers, studio owners, art directors, agency heads, public relations people, editors, designers, and others—to find out the best way to attack different markets.

This book tells you how to handle the business end of photography. That means identifying buyers, learning what they look for in a portfolio, and what you can expect to earn for the job.

The most important part of *The Working Photographer* is, of course, the job: finding it, getting it, and doing it. We show you how to handle the entire process, from contacting the prospective client to negotiating a fee to preparing for the shoot.

We'll tell you how to equip yourself with hardware as well as knowledge and how to inexpensively buy a core system to start working with now and to build on as your business expands.

Freelance photography is covered in detail because it's both the most difficult of the professional photographic options and potentially the most lucrative. The pleasures and perils of running your own business are presented realistically, including business procedures, valuable shortcuts, and how to have the I.R.S. on your side.

The book touches on the major specialities, from advertising to fashion to travel photography. Your natural talents and interest will point you in one of these directions. We've included a simple checklist to help you see how your interests, skills, and personality affect your photographs, so that you can determine what you like to do photographically and then see how this fits into the commercial photography market.

In short, *The Working Photographer* contains the advice we would have liked to receive when we were starting out. It's a combination of everything we've learned about the professional photography business. We wrote it for people who are reaching for success. We think it will give you the head start you need to outdistance your competition.

CHAPTER 1

LOVE OR MONEY?

You love to take photographs. And you're good at it. Your friends say so. Your relatives say so. Most important, *you* say so. In fact, your pictures are so good people sometimes ask you to photograph something or even (hallelujah!) pay you to do so. That's a trend you would like to continue. You want to become a professional photographer.

The big question is, of course: How? What does it take to work as a professional photographer?

As you might have expected, it has a lot to do with making money. People aren't considered professionals until they have been paid to do whatever it is they do. Like an athlete, if you do it only because it's fun, you're an amateur. If you do it because it's fun *and* someone pays you for it, you're a professional.

In photography, making money is a time-honored tradition. Right from the start, photography captured people's imaginations and their dollars. Francs, actually. The first successfully permanent photograph was made by a Frenchman, Nicéphore Niépce, in 1826. Louis Jacques Mandé Daguerre gets most of the credit, however, first because he became Niépce's business partner and, second, because when he discovered a better way to make a photographic image on metal permanent he had the foresight to name the process after himself: the daguerreotype. The French government bought his invention, and Daguerre became the world's first money-making professional photographer.

That's not to say that money is the only thing that separates the amateur from the professional. There's also the issue of skill.

In those early days, photography was complicated, the process slow and inaccurate, and the materials as likely to explode as to create an image. "Quality" photography soon became a matter for professionals. And there were certainly a lot of them. Right away, marketing became a key part of professional photography.

Today, with electronic and computerized cameras, film that develops itself in seconds, and sophisticated photographic techniques available to anyone, what sets the professional apart? Your Aunt Minnie can make use of the same photographic technology that's used by the top photojournalists or fashion photographers: 35mm camera, motor drive, high-speed films, synchronized electronic flash unit. Does that mean that Aunt Minnie can do the same job?

No. Because the picture is only a part of it. Professional photography requires a complex combination of talent, technical skill, business and marketing sense, and commitment. In order to be successful, you need to have a firm grasp on all these.

THE MAKING OF A PROFESSIONAL

There are certain characteristics all professional photographers have in common. Let's look at the most important.

Technical knowledge. All work is expected to be technically perfect, and the photographer to be in total control of his or her equipment and processes—not the other way around.

Organization. From negative files to business records to packing for a location shooting, the professional is in control of thousands of details. It's the details in photography that mean the difference between perfect and useless.

Ability to deliver. There is seldom time or money enough to do a job twice, and so a client expects the professional to get it right the first time. A photographer must be able to solve aesthetic and technical problems quickly, creatively, and within a budget.

Vision. This distinguishes one photographer from another. The way you look at the world and transmit it in pictures is an extension of your personality; it is part of your photographic style. The stronger and more identifiable it is, the more successful you will be. (There are, of course, extremes. Very few brides want their weddings shot with a distorting fish-eye lens, so if that's your view of the world, don't specialize in wedding photography.)

Drive. Without this, nothing happens. In fact, we've seen a few photographers who are weak in everything *except* an all-consuming drive. That alone, in some cases, is enough to make a successful photographer.

WORKING FOR YOURSELF VS. WORKING FOR SOMEONE ELSE

There are two kinds of professional photographers: staff and self-employed (the term includes both freelancers and studio owners). The basic distinction is this: If you're on staff, the people who hired you take care of the business end of things (like getting work, delivering it when it's done, billing, and record keeping); if you're self-employed, you *are* the business and have the responsibility for all aspects of it yourself. There are pros and cons to both.

STAFF PHOTOGRAPHER

- Only one employer; staffer is on company payroll
- Paycheck is regular and there are fringe benefits
- Equipment and materials are provided
- Work is assigned and (somewhat) guaranteed
- Work may become routine
- There's usually a ceiling on earnings
- Advancement may be limited
- Work is usually for newspaper, industry, catalogs, wedding/portrait/yearbook, or audiovisual employers.

SELF-EMPLOYED

- Entrepreneurs do best
- There's no ceiling on earnings
- Advancement is unlimited
- You are free to choose your type of work and clients
- Security and fringe benefits are lacking
- You must provide your own equipment and materials
- High degree of skill is required to break in.

If you want security and a steady income, staff photography

is ideal. Many staff positions provide on-the-job training and can be a rewarding way to gain experience (and some money) before going out on your own. Entry-level jobs paying respectable wages are actually available. Staff jobs at a newspaper or a corporation, for example, can provide a lifetime of interesting and exciting work.

Wayne Lenebaker is a photographer with General Electric in Schenectady, New York. He describes working as a full-time staff photographer:

> The way GE is structured, the various departments within the company can use us or they can go outside. It's up to them....It is a hassle to get outside photographers and have them cleared for some projects. They use us because we are convenient and we do a good job for them. We are basically a service organization.
>
> There are many different areas you can work in. If you're lucky enough or good enough to get involved in an industrial situation, you can do some scientific photography. For instance, we've got one person here who does a lot of laser photography. There is specialization within the group, although a lot of it is passed around to give others some experience.
>
> I would say that 99 percent of learning the different aspects of photography depends on experience. Of course, every industrial situation is a unique setup and you gear yourself to it. To be a good industrial photographer you have to be a jack-of-all-trades. If an assignment comes down the pike to shoot a "grip-and-grin"—that's an award or presentation shot with three or four people—you go out and do that. If it's "Go down and photograph a scientist," or a problem-solving thing, such as shoot a laser and make it colorful—or make it pretty for a brochure—you do that.
>
> One nice aspect of the job is that you do have varied assignments. You really don't know what you'll be doing from one day to the next. Which is kind of neat.

If you want challenge and enjoy running your own show, then go out on your own. According to recent government figures, 40 percent of all photographers in the United States are self-employed. The risks are considerably greater than with a staff job, but so is the potential payoff. You answer to no one but yourself, your client, and the I.R.S., but you stand to make considerably more money because you own the business. Of course, this also means that, in addition to being a great photographer, you must be a marketing genius, an efficient bookkeeper, and a smooth-talking diplomat. A little bit of used-car salesman doesn't hurt, either.

Going straight into freelance photography is usually a disaster. You will do well to spend some time working in a staff job or as an assistant to an established photographer when you first start out.

Part-time beginnings

A third option is do photography only part of the time. Sometimes this is a good way to start because you can learn a field without making a large commitment of time and money. Sometimes it's a way to make a hobby pay off by shooting weddings on weekends for a local studio or on your own.

To really succeed, however, you must make the commitment to full-time photography. Without that, it's nearly impossible to rise above low-paying jobs and establish yourself as a serious professional.

THE PHOTOGRAPHIC SPECIALTIES

Most photographers specialize. That means they choose to work in a particular area of photography. Each specialty requires different skills and different approaches; each delivers different rewards.

Claudio Edinger, author of *Chelsea Hotel* and an award-winning photojournalist, talks about his kind of photography this way:

> I really enjoy all different aspects of photography, philosophical, political, aesthetic.... I always wanted to stay in photojournalism because...I have a tremendous curiosity about the world and I feel photojournalism helps me understand it better. I like to be in touch. I like to know. I can't be satisfied unless I'm doing research...or discovering. It's something that I have inside: I need it.
>
> I moved to New York (from São Paolo), became the correspondent for *Vision* (a Brazilian magazine), and decided to do documentary work about New York City. I saw the Hassidic Jews in the streets, did some research, and saw that

nothing had really been published on them. So I went to their neighborhood, just to see how they live. And I took a camera and started taking pictures. Then ... I let my beard grow, cut my hair very short, and moved into the community to photograph the way they lived.

Even if it's as simple a thing as a portrait of a doctor who saved a child ... there is something special there. This man is a hero and there is an aura around him. I want to understand what this is all about: What made this normal man risk his life to get a poor kid out from under the wheels of the subway? Or if it's Mayor Koch getting an award from the organization of retired seamstresses in Queens. It sounds like a little thing, but it's history happening ... even if it's a little bit of history. It helps explain the world in some way, even if it's a small way.

Marek Milewicz and Majka Lamprecht, New York agents for top fashion photographers, talk this way about some of the qualities that make people successful fashion photographers:

If I had a young guy, I would tell him: Hey, listen, don't think you're going to fly tomorrow, because the competition is tremendous. You really have to work on your style first. It might take you six years; it might take you eight years. You're not going to do *Vogue* [magazine] and Calvin Klein right away. Of course, maybe if you're very talented and you meet some people, you'll get a break. Because luck is also very important in this business. Talent, connections, luck. Everything needs to be there.

Fashion photographers have to be aware of what's going on. They have to feel fashion. If they have a style themselves, they are very good in fashion. You can see it. It is projected in their work. A lot of young people go to Europe and get the sense of fashion there. Young photographers go to Paris or to Milan to work. They don't make much money, but they're in the milieu where a lot of things happen. There are a lot more fashion magazines being published in Europe than there are here. And you have a better chance to work.

Robert McCabe, a successful still-life photographer working on national consumer ads, puts it this way:

When you're doing a fashion shoot, there're always so many people around—all sort of staring over your shoulder. Some of the models can be a bit of a problem. It gets too crazy, too hectic. A still life, by comparison, is something that doesn't talk back to you, doesn't really complain too much, doesn't move too far away. And you can shoot it again ...and again and again and again, until you get it exactly the way you like it.

What I like about still life is the idea of having total control over the situation, whereas when you're doing people—fashion, portraiture, beauty—you don't really have it. Still life is something where you can totally manipulate what goes on in the shot.

Looking at it from the point of view of a business, the opportunity to make money in still life is probably far greater than in some other parts of the business.

Here are the main areas of specialization:

Advertising. This is the most visible, lucrative, and glamorous area of photography. It also has the highest overhead and the most competition.

Editorial. This is photography for publication other than advertising. The rates are lower than those for advertising, but at the top levels they come close. Overhead is usually proportionately lower, and often much lower. It's also what people mean when they talk about "photojournalism" and "documentary reportage," although those are more specialized types of editorial photography.

Portrait. Every town has one studio or more specializing in wedding photography and family and school portraiture. The studios range in size from one-person shops to large operations employing many photographers. In small markets, these studios may also do advertising and editorial work.

Corporate/industrial. This well-paid field covers many types of photography for business and industry. In style it combines advertising and journalism, but in payment can be more like advertising.

Scientific and medical. Small, very technical, highly specialized fields, these are mostly peopled by full-time staff photographers. Salaries can be quite good, and entry-level positions usually offer on-the-job training on sophisticated equipment. Require either prior knowledge of the discipline in which you want to work or the ability to acquire it quickly.

There are many subspecialties within these broad categories. A comprehensive list and brief description of some of them follows.

Still life. As in painting, this describes a picture of something that doesn't move—any inanimate object. Most photographs you see in advertisements are still-life shots of the client's product. A bottle and glass of Miller's, a pack of Marlboro's, an RCA TV set, or a digital-disk player—all are still life. Aside from clothes, catalogs consist mostly of still-life photographs.

Still lifes are always done in the controlled lighting conditions of a studio, require a large-format camera, and—depending on the size of the products—a large space. It is primarily used in advertising, and at the top levels it commands very high rates.

Food. This is a specialized type of still-life photography. It is also done in the studio with large-format cameras and controlled lighting. As the name implies, however, it deals only with food—cooked and raw—photographed for ads, cookbooks, magazine features, packaging, menus, displays, etc.

Two factors complicate food photography: the need to work always with real food, and the requirement that it look more attractive than in real life. Food photographers or someone on their staff will search all the vegetable sections in town for perfectly ripe, unbruised tomatoes in the middle of January—that sort of thing. But the aggravation is usually assuaged by the rates, which are high.

A food photographer will often work with a home economist—an invaluable asset because they know how to cook and present food so that it photographs in a most appealing way.

When you're starting out, the budget for a shot may not be big enough to include a home economist. In that case, the client can sometimes send a person who knows the product and can do the cooking, cutting, and arranging that's needed to make an appetizing photo. Or, if it's a really small job, maybe you can con your spouse into it. (In our family, the photographer is also the cook; so that has never worked.)

Illustration. This is a tableau, a little slice of life that is designed to sell the client's product or service. It usually involves a set or location (indoor or outdoor), models, and lots of props. As examples of illustration photography, look at ads for Salem cigarettes (people having a good time with cigarettes), Coke and Pepsi (people having a good time with soft drinks), Maxell tapes (people being blown away by music).

Illustration photography can be done with any camera format, but the most common are 35mm and 6×6 cm (2¼ inch square). Powerful electronic flash units are the light source most often used. A large and elaborately equipped studio is usually required. If a location outside the studio is used, the set must still be illuminated and "propped" (furnished). The photographer needs to be a director, because you're working with models to create a brief piece of theater. You must be good with people and able to stay in control of a lot of things happening at once.

It also pays very well, and it may allow you to travel to exotic places with beautiful models—where you then get up at dawn and work into the evening to keep to the client's schedule. (It is fun, but not for the reasons you'd think.)

Fashion. This is obvious. It's clothes and accessories, either on models or by themselves as a fashion still life. Fashion is done either in the studio or on location and can be shot with any format. The format of choice is 35mm with electronic flash lighting when models are involved because it captures mood and movement. (Where such situations have been shown in television and films, the atmosphere is characterized by a whirring motor drive and the photographer's comments of "Great...that's beautiful...lovely..." In this case, the movies pretty much have it right.)

Fashion photography is used in advertising, catalogs, brochures, and editorial contexts. The rates are usually high, but they vary widely according to the client, the area of the country you're working in, and the eventual use of the photographs. Advertising is the highest; editorial and catalog are the lowest.

Beauty. These photographs are usually for cosmetic ads and are closeups of faces, hands, legs, etc. Beauty is set apart from fashion photography by the type of lighting and its focus on faces rather than on clothes, but the equipment is similar to that used to photograph fashion. Think of it as still lifes of people. Rates, once again, are high but vary according to use: You can charge more for a national ad than for a department-store flyer.

Special effects. Here the lighting, camera, and film are manipulated in ways that register an image that was never in front of the lens. Or at least not all at once. This type of photography is characterized by things that glow like neon, streaks of color trailing from an object, laserlike effects, people and things floating in space, and other phenomena.

The result is an unusual and often surreal image. It requires considerable technical ability and specialized equipment. Done well, it can be used by almost any client, and it will usually garner a premium price.

Corporate. Photographing for business and industry—products, people, and working situations. It includes annual reports, industrial advertising (as opposed to consumer—we'll explain this in Chapter 3), corporate brochures and magazines, audiovisual (a large percentage, anyway), and portraits of executives.

The usual format is 35mm or 2¼ in. square and is done on location in business offices, warehouses, docks, factories, and other places where the lighting is less than ideal. Corporate photography requires a control of existing light or the ability to light any location quickly and accurately.

Rates vary from very high for annual reports to midrange for brochures to low for public relations and company newsletters.

Frequently, well-paying staff jobs are available in corporate photography.

Architectural. The photography of the interiors and exteriors of buildings. Examples of this kind of work appear in magazines like *Architectural Digest, Domus* (an Italian magazine), *House and Garden,* or even *House Beautiful.*

Architectural photography is usually done with large-format cameras (4 × 5) with wide-angle lenses and adjustments ("tilts" and "swings") that keep perspective lines straight and all edges in focus in the resulting picture. Lighting for interiors is perhaps the most difficult of all. It requires specialized equipment and the ability to blend existing light with photo lights to create mood and the sense of place. The markets are primarily magazines, architectural firms, designers, construction companies, and any concern supplying items shown either outside or in an interior (furniture, fabrics, paint, flooring, siding, etc.).

Photojournalism. Tells a story in photographs, with or without an accompanying text. This specialty requires an eye for what's newsworthy or has human interest. In many instances, it requires daring and a willingness to go where nobody in their right mind wants to be (with the guerrillas in some jungle outpost, for instance). A true photojournalist perks up at the mere mention of a situation like that.

It is not always necessary to risk your life, however. Many journalists happily create feature stories for various magazines. For examples, check out magazines like *Life, People, Geo, Omni, Rolling Stone, Arizona Highways, National Geographic,* etc.

The format is 35mm, with a minimum of lighting equipment. Black and white used to be the medium of choice, but color is what sells now.

Travel. This isn't limited to photography of "faraway places with strange-sounding names." The local resort area or a canoe trip to the next town are travel photography, too. But in all cases, travel photography must make the place look good enough to be worth traveling to.

This specialty appeals to many beginners because everybody has either been someplace that would make a good travel or vacation picture-story or would like to go. That's what makes this field so competitive. It is an excellent opportunity to sell photographs you already have in your files ("stock photography").

The markets are usually national and regional magazines, special-interest magazines (travel, airline, and chamber-of-commerce publications), newspapers, book publishers, and publishers of posters, calendars, and greeting cards.

Nature and wildlife. This is exactly what it sounds like: photography of anything in nature (landscapes, plants, animals, and closeups of rocks and trees). It requires an interest in nature and some scientific knowledge about the subject, as well as a considerable amount of precision and patience.

The format is usually 35mm, but larger formats are preferred for certain subjects (such as landscapes) and markets (such as posters). To photograph elusive wildlife in low-light conditions, you will also need fast, long lenses and, sometimes, specialized lighting or remote-triggering rigs.

In general, the markets for nature and wildlife, like those for travel, are special-interest magazines and book publishers who deal with those subjects.

Sports. This includes everything and anything that someone has defined as a sport, from the common ones like baseball and football to more exotic ones like surfing and hang gliding. It requires knowledge and love of sports to be able to anticipate the action and be in the right place to get the best shots.

Since speed and mobility are important, sports photographers use 35mm cameras equipped with long, fast lenses.

The primary market is newspapers and magazines (national, regional, and sports-specialty), stock files, and advertising. In addition, teams, sponsors, and participants are always interested in good action photographs.

Medical and scientific. This highly technical photography documents scientific research and medical proceedings. To see excellent examples of this specialty, look at any of Lennart Nilsson's photographs of the fetus developing in the womb. It requires highly sophisticated equipment, specialized training, and close working relationships with research scientists and physicians and/or institutions. Usually staff members of laboratories, re-

Specialty	Description	Use
Still Life (Tabletop, Product Photography)	Product shots in a studio. People may sometimes be included, but the product is always the most important element.	• General advertising • All media • Catalog
Illustration	A dramatization of an idea to sell a product or illustrate a magazine story. Very theatrical in approach. Mostly studio, but some location. T.V. commercials that don't move.	• General advertising • Editorial
Food	A special branch of still life. Appetizing pictures of *real* food. Smaller market than products, but you'll never starve.	• Catalog • General advertising • Editorial
Fashion	Beautiful (usually) clothes, shoes, and accessories on models or by themselves. About 70% studio, 30% location. Top people travel to exotic places.	• Catalog • General advertising • Editorial

search institutions, universities, or hospitals handle the needed scientific photography.

In some cases, large corporations require highly specialized technical photography to document specific products or processes. Breaking into these specialties often requires taking a staff job and being trained within the organization.

Bought by	Rates	Over-head	Skills	Equipment
Advertising agencies, sometimes directly by advertisers, design houses.	VH	VH	• Studio lighting • Patience • Work under pressure • Small-set design • Propping • Work from layout	• 4 x 5–8 x 10 • Polaroid back • Studio strobes or incandescent (tungsten) lights • Medium to large studio
Advertising agencies, magazines.	VH	VH	• Intricate lighting of large sets or locations • Direction of models to create mood • Set design • Nerves of steel	• 2¼–35mm • Lots of lights • Large studio • Facilities for set construction
Advertising agencies, magazines.	H	H	• Specialized lighting • Appreciation of food and its presentation • Preparation techniques (usually handled by a home economist) • Speed	• 4 x 5–8 x 10 • Same as still life but with well-equipped kitchen
Advertisers, design houses	H	H	• Very Stylized light • Ability to create mood appropriate to clothes • Good studio lunches • Calm in the midst of chaos	• 2¼–35mm • Appropriate lights • Studio with dressing room • Limo • Mirror

Portrait. This specialty includes such subspecialties as formal portraits of business executives, individual and family portraits in the home or studio, or photographs of babies and pets. The most important qualification is the ability to work with people and get them to relax in front of a camera. When photographing babies and pets, it simply needs more in the way of

Specialty	Description	Use
Beauty	Faces and hands of beautiful women, usually to sell cosmetics.	• General advertising • Editorial • Catalog
Special Effects	Creating, in the studio, unusual, startling, or surreal images. Some staff jobs in AV houses.	• General advertising • Editorial • AV
Corporate/ Industrial	All phases of business, from top management portraits to factory operations and product applications to public relations must be photographed at one time or another. Freelancers travel often (usually to Holiday Inns in Georgia). Very little studio work. Staff jobs available.	• Annual report • AV • Brochure • Advertising • Newspaper • Magazines
Architectural	Photographing exteriors and interiors of buildings in their best light.	• General advertising • Editorial

props and acting from the photographer. (It may look silly to the parents, but funny hats on the photographer *will* make a baby look up and smile.)

You will need a medium-format camera (6×6 cm—that is, 2¼ in. square—or many use 6×7 cm), a medium-long ("portrait"

Bought by	Rates	Over-head	Skills	Equipment
Advertising agencies, magazines.	H–M	H–M	• Very flattering use of light and angle • Mastery of subtle color	• 2¼–35mm • Strobe • Appropriate screens, reflectors • Small studio
Advertising agencies, magazines, design houses, AV houses.	H–M	H–M	• Complex lighting and camera setups • Design and rigging of props and effects	• 35mm–8 x 10 • Animation camera (Forox, etc.) • Specialized lights and other bits and pieces • Nothing is really standard
Large and small companies, design houses, AV, advertising agencies.	M	M–L	• Work with all kinds of people • Color-correct existing light • Make *anything, anywhere* look good (at least to the client) • Work fast	• 35mm–2¼ • Powerful portable flash
Advertising agencies, architects, designers, landscape architects, magazines.	M–H	M	• High sense of design • Careful, complex lighting of interiors • Subtle use of natural light on exteriors • Mastery of large camera on location	• 4 x 5 • Wide-angle lenses • Variety of portable lights

length) lens, and studio lighting (either "hot" incandescent lights or a studio electronic flash outfit). You also need a very good knowledge of portrait lighting techniques.

Weddings. These are usually handled by the same studios that specialize in portraits, although it is possible to photograph

Specialty	Description	Use
Portrait/ Wedding	Creates individual and group portraits for all occasions, including weddings and other family events. May also do school portraits. Some staff jobs in larger studios.	• Wall • Album • Yearbook • Newspaper
Medical/ Scientific	Photography to record medical or other scientific procedures; diagnostic and research applications. Highly technical, often macro- or micro-photography. Usually staff job.	• Documen- tation • Editorial • Research
Photo-journalism	Shooting news and feature pictures as well as picture stories. Ability to write helps, but not required. Most newspaper jobs are staff. Most magazine jobs are freelance.	• All editorial markets
Travel	Pictures and picture stories of interesting, often exotic people and places.	• Editorial • Advertising • AV

weddings on a freelance or part-time basis. Use the same medium-format camera, with an additional lens or two. Most wedding photographers also use relatively fast, powerful strobes (on-camera electronic flash units).

In any case, the photographer's main responsibility is to

Bought by	Rates	Over-head	Skills	Equipment
Individuals, schools.	M–L	M–L	• Work well with subjects • Produce flattering but convincing pictures	• 2¼ format • Studio lighting • Powerful camera-mounted flash • Studio
Usually staff photos but some bought by specialized publications.	M	H–VH	• Use of sophisticated equipment • Knowledge of scientific field in which you work • Ability to cope with medical/lab environment	• Varies widely, usually supplied
All editorial markets.	M–L	M–L	• Deep interest in people and events • Dedicated to work • Work fast • Travel light • Resourceful • Know when to run	• 35mm • Long, fast lenses • Small, fast flash
Magazines, advertising agencies, advertisers, newspapers, AV houses.	M–L	M–H	• Ability to see same place a new way • Get along with people in any language • Strong digestive system • Ability to get along without lost baggage	• 35mm • Small flash

record a rare and—for those directly involved—very important event and to make everybody look better than they ever have. You are working for demanding clients in an emotionally charged situation; so good humor and diplomacy are essential. You must also know the standard wedding poses, so that you will be able to

Specialty	Description	Use
Nature/Wildlife	Single images and picture stories of beautiful places and interesting animals.	• Editorial • Calendars
Sports	Exciting images of everything from auto racing to zebra polo.	• Editorial • Advertising

deliver the sort of photographs the family wants to look at in their album year after year.

A good knowledge of the merchandising that's involved—multiple prints, enlargements, albums, special effects—will contribute to your financial success in this specialty.

The specialties and the markets are, of course, not always as clearly defined as stated in this small space. Depending on the geographical region you work in, the size of the market, the kind

Bought by	Rates	Over-head	Skills	Equipment
Magazines, paper products	M–L	M	• Knowledge of subjects • Willingness to live in the woods for long periods of time • Keep equipment working in hostile environment	• 35mm • Long, fast lenses for wildlife
Magazines, newspapers, teams, advertising agencies.	M–H	M	• Speed • Ability to anticipate action • Knowledge of sports • Ability to dodge flying players as well as assorted balls, pucks, raquets	• 35mm • Long, fast lenses

of clients you have, and the range of your personal interests, specialties will frequently overlap. Small markets will need a photographer who can do almost everything, while in big cities people expect more specialization. Use these categories as a guide, though, as you're deciding what area (or areas) of photography to pursue.

As a quick reference, we've included a chart showing the specialty, who buys it, the kind of equipment and skills required, and the comparative range of rates and overhead costs.

BREAKING IN... Peter B. Kaplan

Peter B. Kaplan is a New York City photographer who has made a national reputation by specializing in dramatic shots from and of the tops of bridges, skyscrapers, and the Statue of Liberty.

I always believed in self-assignment. Most guys just sit around and wait for that phone to ring. If I wasn't doing anything I'd be out shooting and climbing, and that's what I think I'm about. I remember standing under the Verrazano-Narrows Bridge and looking up and wondering, *"What's it like to be on top of those towers? Someday I want to go up there."* That was the start of my fascination with climbing and photographing these places.

To get work, I pounded the pavements. I'd call an editor to show them my work. It takes two, three months to get through to an editor. You've got to keep calling and calling. You've got to be persistent. It took lots of phone calls to get published. You get, "We're all away this week, call next week." Or, "We're really in a panic—call back in two weeks." So you call them in two weeks and it's something else. You get to the point of being a pest. "Oh, that guy again. Sure, why don't you come in on Wednesday?" So you show up and you get, "Mr. Jones will be tied up in a meeting all afternoon." So what do you do? You want to get published. You keep at it until it finally works. And it *will* eventually work.

Assisting is one of the greatest ways of learning photography. You learn from the masters—"masters" being those that are successful, those that are in business. A lot of the ones I worked for lasted a year or less, some of them went on to become very successful, very famous photographers. I think when I worked for them...I had the formula: Put all your effort into it; make it the best job that you can. That's why I was a successful assistant.

I assisted for nine-and-a-half years for 134 different photographers. The very first and last photographer I worked for were the same guy. I learned about self-promotion when I was an assistant. I was a pioneer in making being an assistant into a business. Assisting is not the place to be if you just want to make money. But in the beginning, you're rough and have a lot of sharp edges. Until you get those smoothed out, you pay your dues.

Self-promotion is anything that makes people think of
you. People remember me through *Moon over Manhattan*.
[This was a self-promotion postcard of a construction
worker "mooning" the photographer on top of New York
City's World Trade Center TV tower with all Manhattan as a
backdrop.] Good self-promotion doesn't necessarily always mean that you're going to get a job. But people
remember you. If you're going after certain jobs, then your
self-promotion has to be geared that way.

I don't think a young photographer should worry about
getting published in the beginning. Play with the camera.
Get to know it. People think photography is so easy. Pick
up a camera, pull it back, push a button here, put it to your
eye and *wham*—you get a shot. Sure you do. You get an
image. But to get a *photograph,* you have to work hard
and get a little bit of your own vision in there.

CHAPTER 2

FINDING YOUR PHOTOGRAPHIC SPECIALTY

*I, like many another boy, burst into the world of photography
with a box Brownie, which I used for taking holiday
snapshots. . . . Gradually, I set myself to try to discover the
various ways in which I could play with a camera. From the
moment that I began to use the camera and to think about it,
however, there was an end to holiday snaps and silly pictures
of my friends. I became serious. I was on the scent of
something . . .*

—HENRI CARTIER-BRESSON,
The Decisive Moment

The two most important things to consider before making
that first phone call to get work are: where you are now and where
you want to be. It's like planning a trip. Before you can select a
route, you have to know your starting point and what the possible
destinations are.

Some photographic specialties will fit your personality, talents, and goals; others will give you nothing but problems. If
you've been photographing for a while you already have a sense of
which type of photography is most appealing to you. The following exercise will give you a good idea of where your natural ability
best fits with professional photography. It will reveal what you
really like to photograph, what you're good at, and what kind of
photographic work fits in best with your unique interests. In
other words, what your starting point is.

TEST YOUR PREFERENCES

If you pay attention to it, this exercise will save you years of trying any kind of photographic job that comes along rather than going after the ones you'll be most successful with.

STEP BY STEP

Step 1. Gather together every photograph—prints, contact sheets, slides, everything—you have ever shot. Now, this is going to look like a monumental undertaking and, if you've been shooting long, it might even be intimidating. But trust us. We promise it will be worth it.

Step 2. Begin at the beginning, earliest pictures first, and look at everything (yes, *everything*). Take as much time as you need; this is supposed to be fun. Try to identify patterns and directions in your work. Look for a style. You do have one—some are more developed than others—and it's in there someplace.

Step 3. Go back and look through the pictures again, this time as objectively as if you were looking at someone else's work. Pick out the five or ten best images. You can detect style even in this small a number.

Step 4. Answer the following questions about the photographs:

1. The subjects of the pictures I like best are:
   a. people
   b. landscapes
   c. buildings
   d. objects

2. Most of these pictures are:
   a. closeups
   b. medium shots
   c. long shots
   d. extreme closeups

3. Most of these pictures were shot:
   a. indoors
   b. outdoors

4. Most of them were made:
   a. by existing light
   b. by on-camera flash
   c. by studio flash or photoflood lights

5. Most of the pictures were:
   a. set up (posed)
   b. not set up (candid)

6. In the photos I selected:
   a. the people are most important
   b. the situation is most important
   c. the composition is most important
   d. the object is most important

This simple quiz has no "right" or "wrong" answers; it's designed just to steer you in the direction of what to look for in your own photographs.

Step 5. Look at your answers. You'll probably see a pattern and some consistency. Your pictures will fit into one of these three basic styles: Personal, Graphic, or Documentary.

Personal style

Your photographs are primarily of people. They are closeups shot either with existing light or added illumination of some kind. They could be portraits of family, friends, or even pets. They could be action shots of people doing things—playing tennis, sharing a joke, hanging around the pool. But in all cases there's a feeling of interaction between the subject or subjects and the photographer.

Graphic style

The subject matter of these photographs can be anything: people, buildings, trees—whatever. It is the shape, the design, the structure of the composition that catch your eye.

Documentary style

The photographs are of people at parties, picnics, parades, races, and in other situations where the event—what is happening or what people are doing—is of primary interest. Although composition is important, it amplifies the situation; it isn't important as a thing in and of itself. These photographs can be made indoors or outdoors, but they are usually done by whatever light is available.

WHERE YOU FIT INTO PROFESSIONAL PHOTOGRAPHY

The basic characteristics that determine your personal style also point you in the direction of a photographic specialty. Unless there are some very strong reasons for it (your uncle left you a million dollars in his will if you devote your life to documenting the architecture of his hometown, for example), don't choose a specialty that's radically different from your personal style. If your photographs are of people in the great outdoors, you won't find happiness photographing meticulously arranged, perfectly lighted beer bottles in the studio. You *would*, however, be happy photographing that beer being enjoyed at a party or a picnic. In short, work to your strengths. Here's how the specialties fit into the three broad categories of personal, graphic, and documentary:

PERSONAL

Portraiture	Illustration
Fashion	Photojournalism
Beauty	

GRAPHIC

Architecture	Corporate
Still life	Fashion
Food	Beauty
Landscape	Special effects

DOCUMENTARY

Photojournalism	Nature and wildlife
Corporations	Sports
Travel	Science, medicine

Your talent and personal preference are important factors in deciding on the type of photography you want to do. But so is the market you're planning to work in.

In general, the smaller the market the less specialized the photography work you'll get. If you are determined to work only in a specialty like fashion or food, you will probably have to relocate to a large city.

So select the specialty that appeals to you, but keep an open mind about it as you read on and learn more about the market.

BREAKING IN . . . Perry and Wooten

Skip Perry and Peter Wooten are the owners of Picture House, a commercial photo studio in Norwalk, CT.

Peter: We do audiovisual, corporate, industrial, still life, and some food. There's probably a shorter list of what we don't do. We don't do fashion. We don't get involved in print ads.

The work we do is dictated by the area we're in. It's what's available. There are a lot of advertising agencies in the area, but they're very copy [word] oriented and don't use much photography. We work basically with corporations or the graphics departments within corporations.

When we started out, it was kind of a loose partnership. We shared equipment and people that we knew who were giving us work. I would do mostly the studio stuff and Skip would shoot on location.

Skip: Starting a studio is difficult because of all the stuff you need: equipment, rent. There're too many ups and downs, and you can't just say, "Well, I think I'll go borrow a quarter of a million dollars from the bank and open up as a business." If you have some backers that want to long-term you and you try to pay them back over ten years . . . well, you're going to have to hustle to be able to pay that back. We took it slow. Now we can go to the bank and get loans, but in the beginning they wouldn't talk to us. We started this business with no investment.

Peter: When you're working with agencies, you've usually got people with you on the shoot who understand what you're doing. That's not always the case when you work directly with corporations. Sometimes it takes a lot of explaining. Everything is done over the phone. There's a lot more responsibility on you. You don't have an art director sitting right there; you can't just hold the cable release and say, "Okay?" to him and he says, "Okay!" to you and bam, you've got your shot. It's really on you.

Sometimes that works for you. They'll call you back and say: "We didn't give you enough input. In a way, this is good, but we want to see it another way." We've shot jobs over [again] four times because of the simple fact that they just can't spring somebody [free] to come on the shoot; we just charge more for the additional shots.

Skip: A lot of the companies, especially the ones out here, are trying to keep their people from going into the city... from dealing too much with New York City agencies. They're trying to keep more of the work in-house. It has met with varying degrees of success. But this attitude means that our market out here is growing. We're getting more work, and more different kinds of work.

Our biggest nemesis is when it gets to be about 6 or 7 o'clock, it's the end of a long day of shooting, and the client will say: "We're really not sure of this and we really need it tomorrow. So, can you shoot it both ways? Just give me a different angle." They don't realize how much work that "different angle" will take. But the reason they say that is that they're not even sure of the title. Is the title going to be three words and take up the top two thirds of the picture? Maybe it'll be one third. You'd better have an alternative. They want to go to the meeting with two shots—"If you don't like this, we've got something else."

CHAPTER 3

HOW THE BUSINESS WORKS

Now that you've decided to become a professional photographer: Welcome to marketing! (Did you think knowing how to take good pictures was enough?)

Any business consists of a buyer and a seller. Simple. Marketing is the way you find the buyers and convince them to buy your product or service, and that simple concept is the basis on which billions of dollars are spent every year for all kinds of advertising and promotion. If you market *yourself* well, you'll be on the receiving end for some of those dollars.

As a professional photographer, you're looking for the people who buy the kind of photography you do. How well you can find them, get them to look at your work, and convince them to hire you will make you or break you as a professional photographer. One thing is sure: They will *not* come looking for you. That's the tough side of the business. The good side is that there are a lot of buyers and a lot of business.

If the first rule of successful photography is *Know thyself*, the second is *Know thy buyer.* Your best bet is to be well informed about the businesses that buy photographs. This chapter introduces some businesses that are good markets for photographers, the kind of photography they use, and who actually buys the work.

Some of these businesses also represent opportunities for photographers interested in staff positions. There are no hard-and-fast rules about which businesses will keep a photographer in-house, but busy agencies, large corporations, public relations firms, audiovisual production houses, and even factories that may have a company paper and need PR photos are likely candidates.

The best way to find out if any of these businesses have a photographic department is to telephone. When you get the switchboard or receptionist, just ask for the photo department or, if that's a dead end, ask for the graphics department or, as a final attempt, public relations. (Remember that this is just investigative. Don't ask *any* of them if they are looking for any new photographers—it's just too tempting for them to say No. If a place does have staff photographers, find out more about that particular company (as explained in Chapter 6), how to present yourself as a professional (see Chapter 7), and then call back to make an appointment to see the appropriate person.

ADVERTISING AGENCIES

TYPE OF PHOTOGRAPHY USED   Still Life ▪ Food ▪ Illustration ▪ Fashion ▪ Beauty ▪ Special Effects ▪ Portraits

What they do

A business or corporation hires an advertising agency to promote their products or services to potential customers. This promotion can include anything from advertising in newspapers, magazines, television, and radio, to billboards, sales brochures, catalogs, and direct mail. They'll use skywriting if it works for the client. And, except for the radio and skywriting, they use some kind of photography for most of the jobs they handle.

Agencies, like photographers, tend to specialize. Some agencies stick to straight ads; some do only collateral (that's brochures, catalogs, exhibits, etc.); others do everything. Generally, agencies—again like photographers—tend to be more specialized in large urban areas where there are more clients and so more demand for each specialty.

Generally, most agencies are considered either consumer-oriented or industrial. For example, Coca-Cola, Jordache, Maytag, and Ivory Soap represent *consumer* accounts. So do most of the ads you see on TV and in popular magazines. On the other hand, large machinery, jet engines, electrical parts, building materials—the kinds of manufactured goods that are primarily sold to other corporations—are *industrial* accounts and are handled by agencies that specialize in that type of business.

Outside the major advertising agency centers of New York and Chicago, the distinctions tend to blur and agencies are not as specialized. This is not to slight Atlanta, Dallas, Houston, Los Angeles, Boston, or Miami—all important cities in terms of advertising, both creatively and financially—but New York and Chicago are still the power centers of American advertising.

There's another advertising distinction you should be aware of: trade advertising. All this means is that the ad (or brochure or whatever) is intended for an audience other than the general public. It could be advertising heavy-industry products to engineers or microfilm to librarians or BMWs to doctors; but it is considered *trade* advertising when it is directed toward a specific population of professionals. This distinction between general interest and trade advertising affects how much you can charge for your photography. (See? And you thought this wasn't interesting.)

The size of an agency also affects the kind of advertising it handles. The smaller the agency, the less specialized it is in terms of both clients and the work it does for them.

Best bets

The less-specialized agencies that do a wide variety of work are better bets for a beginner than the ones which do strictly national advertising campaigns. They have a wider variety of photo assignments and are more likely to have jobs with lower budgets on which they would be willing to try out a newcomer. If you do well, you advance to better work and bigger agencies.

Before approaching an ad agency for photographic work, look first at its clients. If you want to photograph fashion models, don't waste your time with an agency that handles tractor and fertilizer accounts. Find one that uses your kind of work, and then concentrate your energy on getting work from them. (We'll tell you how to find out which agency does what in Chapter 6.)

Inner workings

Since it doesn't hurt to be as knowledgeable as possible about the people you're working for, here's how a typical ad agency gets work done:

[The speaker is Beth Patterson Tooni, who has been an account executive with Marstellar in New York City and General Electric's in-house agency.]

It's my responsibility as an account executive to talk with the person who is responsible for the advertising at the client's [end]. I would be the liaison between the client and the agency, but he would be the liaison between the product manager [at the client] and me.

We would sit with the client's advertising manager and the product manager and just listen ... to what they wanted in the ad, information about the product, that kind of thing. Then ask all kind of questions and decide on what approach would work best.

Back at the agency, I would sit down with the art director on the account, the copy person on the account, and, possibly, the creative director if the ad were the least bit unusual. At the beginning of a series of ads, we would establish how much space is devoted to copy, what the visual is, the look of the ad, that kind of thing.

The client would then approve a comp [comprehensive design] with headlines and a copy block [space for text]. If a photograph were to be used, it would probably be sketched.

When you get to shooting the ad, you *always* shoot it the way you said you were going to shoot it. And then, if you get a better idea on the spot, you shoot it that way also.

It wasn't [as though] one art director had one photographer that he'd always use. It would be kind of a collaboration. If one art director had been having good luck with a photographer, another would come up and ask him, "Hey, who do you think we could use for this shot?" And they'd recommend photographers back and forth among them.

The most important thing in any trade ad is the photograph. It's what's going to get the magazine reader to stop and look at it. It'd be nice to think a good headline is going to do it, but it's not. If the photograph isn't good, if it isn't attention-getting, if it isn't unusual to some extent, the ad's not going to be any good.

Who buys photography?

The art director (A.D.) handles the buying of photography and is the person to whom to show your portfolio. Large agencies have more than one art director, and often each is working on only one account. If you've done your research, you can ask for the A.D. who handles the account you're most interested in. And if one art director won't see you or doesn't have work for you, ask to be referred to someone else.

Some very large agencies have art buyers. These are the people who look at portfolios for the art directors. They then keep names on file and recommend them to agency art directors as needed. They also negotiate price and serve as a quality control on the work that's been done.

Other agency people can recommend a photographer, but don't really have the final say. (Some recommendations are taken more seriously than others—from the client, for example.)

DESIGN STUDIOS

TYPE OF PHOTOGRAPHY   Still life ▪ Corporate ▪ Illustration ▪ Food ▪ Beauty ▪ Fashion ▪ Special Effects ▪ Architectural ▪ Portrait ▪ Medical and Scientific (if studio specializes in that work)

What they do

It's easiest to describe a design house by starting with what it does not do: It does not place ads or create advertising campaigns—that's the major difference between it and an advertising agency. It does design and produce brochures, packaging, annual reports, corporate "identity," exhibits, posters, and other promotional materials. The design studio generally works directly with its clients, primarily corporations and businesses, to develop these.

Often a design house will specialize in annual reports or exhibitions. These are excellent markets for a photographer.

Best bets

Design studios range in size from one guy with a drawing board to a large organization with many designers on staff. Like advertising agencies, the smaller ones will be more likely to take a chance on a new photographer because the budgets on the jobs are smaller and less is at stake. Design studios revolve around the style and personality of the president/founder, the designer at the top who has usually built the business on the basis of an individual talent and reputation.

Because each studio has a distinctive style, it's a good idea to look at examples of work beforehand to see how your style meshes with its. It also pays to adapt your portfolio or "book" (see Chapter 7) more closely to the kind of work the studio produces— but only if you're interested in doing that kind of work. (If the studio's style is New Wave and you like to shoot Old Guard portraits, don't even approach them unless you're ready to make that drastic a change.)

Who buys photography?

In most design studios of any size, even though there may be a hierarchy of art directors, designers, and board people, the name on the door usually makes the decision on hiring photographers. Therefore, try to get to see the owner/designer directly to show your work. Some studios will have a drop-off policy—ask you to leave your portfolio to be looked at at their leisure. Some will see everybody, just to see what new talent they can find.

MAGAZINES

TYPE OF PHOTOGRAPHY   Photojournalism ▪ Nature and Wildlife ▪ Travel ▪ Architectural ▪ Fashion ▪ Beauty ▪ Medical and Scientific ▪ Corporate

What they do

All magazines have two basic concerns: editorial and advertising. Editorial is the reason for their existence; advertising keeps them alive. Here, we're addressing editorial: the stories and photographs that make up the heart of the magazine.

Readers buy the magazine for its editorial content. This in turn boosts its circulation, which in turn lets it raise the rate it can charge for the advertising. The photographs in any magazine are either commissioned (they sent someone out to take them), or bought from a freelancer (someone came to the office with a ready-made picture story). In some cases, especially travel or news, photos to illustrate an existing story are bought from a stock photo agency. Any photograph a magazine buys must fit with the editorial policy and the theme of the magazine.

Inner workings

Ross Baughman, Pulitzer-Prize-winning photojournalist, operates a photo agency called Visions. Here, he talks about selling pictures and photostories to magazines:

The most valuable thing a freelancer brings to any editor is an idea. Any editor obviously has a whole Rolodex full of qualified photographers, some of whom have been their friends for a number of years. They certainly have their first lines of loyalty.

In the beginning, a magazine freelancer is going to have to take the first risks. They're going to have to shoot on speculation. I would suggest a long, meaningful essay which keeps their motivation high throughout. Subject matter about which they can have a good attitude; that they care about; that has substance. And that also has a timeliness and then, almost ironically, a timelessness.

The main idea is to interest editors by showing them something they haven't seen before. We don't want to see any more stories about the bum on the corner or about drug abuse and runaways. Those are overdone. But there's a whole range of domestic stories. You don't have to go to Timbuktu to take photographs. You can find subjects in your own backyard: stories about the direction the American family is going and what's happening to the American dream, for example.

The format of a query letter is not ironclad, because all you're trying to offer is an intriguing, compelling headline for a story. In fact, at best the letter shouldn't be any more than 20 or 30 words—dramatic words, almost like the eleven o'clock news. You have to interest the editor. You've got to come up with a well-researched, specific proposal and put some little twist to it, something that makes it different from the newspaper headlines. You've got to come up with something that will still seem fresh by the time it's completed, by the time it's laid out, by the time it's on the newsstand, three months or four months down the road.

I want to emphasize how important a personal, one-time meeting can be if you can arrange it—even though some editors are at a loss for time and just want you to drop off your work. High-quality work is only part of the battle: The editors want to know if they can work with you; they want to size you up; they want to gauge your enthusiasm and see and hear what your ideas are.

Best bets

General-interest magazines like *Life* are few; they have been replaced with a wealth of special-interest magazines that cover every topic from animals to zeppelins. So there are probably a lot more magazines out there than you think, and at least one will be eager to publish your photographs. Chances are, this won't at first be one of the better paying magazines, and your friends may even have to write to the editor for copies—but publication *is* publication. And you can go on to bigger and better things from there. Also, if you have an interesting story or an impressive portfolio, don't be afraid to tackle the well-known national magazines. They *must* fill the pages with new, exciting stories and photographs every month. You might just hit them at the right time with the right idea.

Who buys photography?

Finding magazines that may be interested in your work requires two steps. First, research your area of interest in *Standard Rate and Data* (see Chapter 6), then get a copy of the magazine you are interested in by either writing to the publisher or browsing through a well-stocked newsstand.

To locate the person who buys photography, check the masthead. Every magazine has a list of all the people responsible for producing the magazine printed near the front of each issue. Look for the picture editor or the features editor. Be very familiar with the magazine before you ever consider calling them for photographic work (more on this in Chapter 6).

NEWSPAPERS

TYPE OF PHOTOGRAPHY   Photojournalism ▪ Sports ▪ Travel

What they do

There are three kinds of newspapers: daily national papers (like *U.S.A. Today, Christian Science Monitor, The National Ob-*

server), daily local/regional papers, and weekly papers (usually suburban or small-town). The first two carry world, national, and local news; the weeklies concentrate on local "soft" news (features on the crafts fair, high school sports, town politics). They represent three very different markets for the photographer.

The "big-time" dailies have staff photographers. If they have a need in another city, they will call a "stringer" (an independent who does regular work for them in that area) or one of the wire services. The regional dailies, reporting local news, also use staff photographers almost exclusively. But either kind of paper can be interested if you happen to be on the spot when something newsworthy happens. You could sell them your photographs of the event because they would not have had time to get a staff photographer there. Call the paper as soon as you have shot your pictures. If they are interested, they will usually have you bring the film in to the newspaper's offices. They will process the film quickly and buy what they want on the spot. If you get to them fast enough, you can sell them the photograph, and get an "in" with them as well as a credit line.

Inner workings

Stephen Shames, a freelance photojournalist and winner of the Leica Medal of Excellence, describes what a newspaper expects from a photographer:

> You have to tell them, Number One, that you have a clear vision and these are the things that you can handle and, Number Two, that you are willing to do anything. You don't care if it's a half-day of a press conference; the idea is to get published.

> One mistake that people make is that everyone goes to *Time* magazine. It's a great place to work, but everyone else is trying to work there, too. There are all these smaller magazines and community newspapers. I started out at *The Berkeley Barb*. At the time, if somebody went to them as a student and said, "Hey, I'd like to work for you; I'd like to do some photo essays," they'd get the chance. In return for... working for almost nothing, you could demand a little control over how your pictures were used, which pictures were chosen.

> At a small paper, maybe you'll get a photo page after you've worked there a couple of months and they know you

do good work. You might get yourself some tear sheets that you can show to get other work. When the mayor comes to your part of town, you can photograph him. If there is a political campaign, you can photograph that. You could do a story on a school, or maybe there's a hospital there or something. Use that community newspaper to get access to events that you couldn't get as a freelancer. You can start developing stories in a community. That is exactly what I did at *The Berkeley Barb*. I got access to events, developed a story, and then, when I showed them to *Newsweek* and *The New York Times*, they said, "Oh, wow, this guy can cover an event; he can take a journalistic portrait."

People are going to buy what they've seen. Some people are so literal that if you [show them] a picture of bacon and eggs, they won't give you a shot of *ham* and eggs [to do]. If you have [a sample portrait of] a woman banking executive and they want a woman executive in the textile field, they'll say, "Well, can you do textile people?"

Other people will look at your pictures and say, "This guy did a great job at Woodstock, he could also shoot a rock concert."

You've got to talk to people and point out to them what you can do. What's really important is a feeling of confidence. That you're willing to do anything and you're confident that you can handle it.

Who buys photography?

The newspaper may or may not have a complete masthead. If they don't, call them and ask to speak to either the picture editor, the assignment editor, or the chief photographer. Remember to get a name, so that if you have a photograph that may be of immediate interest (spot news) you can call the editor directly.

As for wages for staff photojournalists, the *Occupational Outlook Handbook* for 1982–83, put out by the United States Department of Labor, states that beginning photographers who worked for newspapers having contracts with the Newspaper Guild had weekly earnings between $175 and $649 in mid-1981, with the majority earning between $250 and $335. Newspaper photographers with some experience (usually four or five years) averaged about $440 a week, the top salary being $678 per week.

PUBLIC RELATIONS COMPANIES

TYPE OF PHOTOGRAPHY   Corporate ▪ Photojournalistic ▪ Portrait ▪ Fashion/Beauty ▪ Food ▪ Scientific ▪ Architectural ▪ Still Life [as client and budget permit]

What they do

The business of a public relations agency is to persuade investors, customers, and the public to view the clients in a favorable light. They will do this through nonadvertising means, such as newspaper and magazine articles, personal appearances by executives and representatives, public projects, speeches, celebrity tie-ins, and so on. It is as serious and profitable a business as advertising, but, because it often masquerades as news, it is a lot less visible as a commercial operation. Public relations activities include the speech made by a Chairman of the Board on the state of the automobile industry, or the ads placed on the editorial page explaining the energy crisis. The function varies from one P.R. organization to another. However, a public relations agency does not ever create ads or brochures to sell a product: They are only selling "image" or reputation.

Best bets

What kind of photography work comes out of this? High volume and low budget, usually. That doesn't mean you should cross P.R. off your list. On the contrary, the public relations market is a wonderful one for a photographer who's starting out, and it can be bread-and-butter to the photographer who's been around awhile. The business covers so wide an area, needs so many different kinds of photography—from the standard grip-and-grin to product shots to portraits of the C.E.O. (and always seems to need them "yesterday")—that there's always work available.

Who buys photography?

The account executive is the person at an agency responsible for all aspects of a client's publicity. Sometimes jobs are handled by someone called a *publicist*. Photography, though important in this field, has a low priority with most agency account executives and publicists. If they're involved in putting together a press conference to announce to the cream of the fashion world their client's new line of jeans, finding the photographer to immortalize the media stars who attend is somewhere in the middle of the list. (*First* on the list is getting the "stars" to show up.) The "stars" get noticed, the event gets noticed, and—by that connection—the company or product gets noticed. The pictures (usually black and white, and usually needed the next morning) will be placed by the agency in various newspapers and magazines. Since publicity agencies don't like to spend time searching for new photographers, they tend to stick with someone they know will come back with printable, competent photographs and who won't scare off any of the famous people.

Once a client starts using you and gets to know they can depend on you, you can be the person they call for all their photographic needs. Don't ever get lazy on a public relations shooting because it's just another politician getting another plaque. You want the agency to think of you as the one who can do more than is asked, rather than as the one who can barely take the easy shots.

If you haven't yet read the interview with the photojournalist in the previous section, do it now. It will make clear how, from the photographer's point of view, P.R. is a marriage of journalistic and corporate work.

AUDIOVISUAL PRODUCTION COMPANIES

TYPE OF PHOTOGRAPHY   Corporate ▪ Photojournalism ▪ Special Effects ▪ Still Life

What they do

Essentially, what audiovisual production companies produce are slide shows: from simple 35mm slides with a sound track at the low end of the scale to multimedia extravaganzas at the high end. These concerns also frequently produce an entire corporate meeting, seminar, trade show, or exhibition. The AV companies range in size from large organizations with writers, graphic designers, and producers on staff to smaller operations, sometimes even just a single person with a large index of useful addresses. The smaller companies staff up with freelancers when a big job comes in.

This large and growing market includes educational filmstrips, executive speech, inexpensive alternatives to film and video in training, product introductions, and even television commercial production using animated slides. Most corporate stockholders' meetings open with some sort of multiprojector audiovisual show, and most executives like to have slides illustrate the points in their speeches (and keep the audience awake).

Best bets

The audiovisual marketplace needs three kinds of photography: product shots (similar to studio still lifes); location shots (telling a visual story by portraying people and places); and graphics artwork and typography photographed with a special camera (Forox, Oxberry, or Marron-Carrol) that can create such special effects as swoops, zooms, or neon glows. The medium uses a lot of slides to get its messages across, particularly in multiprojector shows. A five-minute nine-projector show could use as many as 700 slides and cost $20,000 to $50,000. There's a story about one sales meeting at which a large automobile manufacturer introduced its new models. The audiovisual "opener"—slides, music, an "environment" for the audience, and special effects making the cars appear out of thin air—cost in the neighborhood of a million dollars. (As they say, that's a nice neighborhood!)

The bad news is that this largesse does not filter down to the photographers. A.V. is words, charts, graphics, effects, script, narrators, music, specialized equipment, and a lot of coordination to fit the pieces together. So, although the photography requires the same skills as corporate brochures and annual reports, it doesn't pay as well. The good news is that the work is easier to get. It is not as competitive, and A.V. production houses are often willing to use beginners because they can't afford a well-established photographer.

Some ambitious photographers offer a complete audiovisual service, photographing graphics as well as tabletops (small product shots) and location work. We know of one who does it all with a good 35mm SLR camera, a copy stand, Kodalith high-contrast film, and some color gels. With that setup he produces basic A.V. shows for major corporations. Naturally, doing the whole show increases the photographer's profit considerably.

Who buys photography?

Finding the right contact depends on the size of the business. If it is a large operation, it will have a staff designer or art director who decides which photographers to use. If there is no designer, ask to see the producer. Often, the designer *is* the owner, and so, as in a design studio, the owner hires the photographers. In approaching small A.V. businesses, always start with the top people. It's their business, and they make all the decisions.

A.V. uses a lot of stock photography, and producers will sometimes buy photographs directly from your portfolio to use in a show rather than asking you to shoot them on assignment.

CORPORATIONS

Corporations handle advertising, promotion, public relations, and internal communications through so many channels it's sometimes difficult to pinpoint who actually buys a photographer's services. Some communications are handled by an advertising agency; some are handled in-house; some are handled by a corporate communications department; some by each separate plant or office. Where to start?

It takes a little detective work to figure out what certain titles or names of departments really mean. We've drawn on a lot of different commercial and industrial concerns for information but will illustrate by using one we know well: General Electric. It's fairly typical of very large corporations, and the basics apply to smaller regional and local businesses.

IN-HOUSE ADVERTISING DEPARTMENTS

TYPE OF PHOTOGRAPHY   Corporate ▪ Industrial ▪ Still Life ▪ Much depends on end product: Medical, Scientific, Travel, Sports, Food, Fashion, Beauty

What they do

Most corporations use a number of advertising agencies, design studios, and public relations concerns for national and local advertising, but frequently they will have an in-house advertising department, too. In the case of General Electric, it is a large full-service department; that is, it handles advertising, press relations, brochures, catalogs, A.V. presentations, and technical publications. It is primarily interested in industrial and product still-life photography.

To find out which companies have in-house advertising departments, look in the *Standard Directory of Advertisers* (see Chapter 6 for more about researching your market).

In most cases, in-house agencies will not handle consumer advertising but concentrate on trade advertising and collateral media (brochures, catalogs, and the like).

Who buys photography?

Structure and job titles are much the same as at other ad agencies—account executive, creative director, art director, copywriter, and so forth. The person to contact for photography is the art director.

Getting specific names is tricky. A large in-house agency may be listed in the *Ad Age 500 Largest Advertisers* with the names of key people. (*Ad Age* is the trade magazine of record for the advertising business. See Appendix C for more information.) Otherwise, telephone and ask the receptionist for the name of the senior art director.

Inner workings

Most companies have an advertising department. Sometimes the function is simply to act as liaison with an outside agency, but often the department is responsible for collateral (brochures, catalogs, sales promotion, meetings, trade shows, etc.). The best way to find out whether they use photography is to telephone the company and ask for the advertising manager. Tell him or her what you do and just ask outright whether they ever use that kind of photography. If they don't, ask what kind of photography they *do* use (you don't want to lose possible work because of a misunderstanding of terms) and ask for an appointment to show your work.

Don't be confused by titles. The name "Advertising Department" is most common, but there are a lot of others. At General Electric, for example, the functions are divided among Sales Promotion, Sales Support, Marketing Communications, Product Advertising, Marketing Services, Communications Programs, Product Information, and so on.

Yes, there are nuances of difference in the type of work each department does, but each is a potential buyer of photography. Try to find out exactly what they do before going in for an appointment. The best way is to ask the person you get to talk to. Be diplomatic and professional. It is not smooth to say, "What the hell do you guys do out there, anyway?"

CORPORATE MAGAZINES

TYPE OF PHOTOGRAPHY Photojournalism ▪ Corporate/Industrial

What they do

The corporate magazine is a sophisticated, professional, special-interest magazine for stockholders and employees. The special interest is anything that concerns the company, and it is treated as news, not as advertising. The work is a cross between journalism, public relations, and corporate-image advertising. These magazines pay very well, are generally of high quality, and consequently are an excellent market for a photographer. The better corporate magazines may be as hard to break into as *Time* and *Newsweek*, though. They pay for quality and expect to get it ready-made, not develop it from raw talent.

Inner workings

Steve Harris is the editor of *The Monogram*, the corporate
magazine for General Electric.

> The assignments range all over the field. Some of them
> are very exotic... assignments that photographers would kill
> to get on. Others are very mundane, like photographing an
> executive in his office or taking a photo of somebody with a
> GE product.
>
> There are so many good photographers. I would say that
> I probably see a hundred photographers a year. They call me
> up constantly. There are certain times of the year that we
> simply have to refuse to see them. Usually it's around the
> time we need to get an issue of the magazine out, or the
> annual report is coming out. At certain times of the year we
> get very, very busy.
>
> They'll call and say, "I know somebody that knows you
> and they said I should give you a call." Or they'll just call out
> of the blue and give me a little rundown of who they are. And
> I'm the kind of guy who likes to see everybody because I used
> to be a struggling writer and I know it helps to get your foot
> in the door. I think I'm one of the few who do.
>
> I'm always looking for somebody who is good; with a
> fresh viewpoint. I want to see what their eye is and how they
> view something. I don't care whether it's in print or another
> medium. If they have an interesting eye that I like, I might
> use them. We don't use stock [pre-existing photographs]. I
> like everything in the magazine to be fresh and shot exclu-
> sively for *The Monogram*.
>
> I also look at how the photographers present them-
> selves. Could they handle photographing a GE executive?
> Wherever I send a photographer, it's a reflection of me and
> it's a reflection of *The Monogram*.
>
> When you shoot for a big corporation, this *is* the big
> time. It may not have the prestige of *Time* magazine, but the
> rates are better by a long shot. We have a circulation of
> 200,000 worldwide; so we're looking for good, big-time pho-
> tographers. The beginning photographer [had] better know
> his craft. He'd better know his camera and he'd better know
> lighting. He should go out and try to get jobs at smaller
> magazines at first. I wouldn't take somebody right off the
> street.

A young photographer trying to break in could try some innovative approaches. For example, if they are in a certain geographic area—outside of New York City—they could write to the headquarters and say, "Hey, I'm a photographer based in Biloxi, Mississippi (or whatever) and am available to take photos of your location down here." Of course, make sure the company you're contacting has business in the area. Research that company. Send some samples. Timing is, of course, important, as it is any time you approach a magazine.

Who buys photography?

Copies of corporate magazines are available from the public relations departments of the companies. For the name of such magazines and their editors, refer to *Working Press of the Nation, Volume V: Internal Publications Directory*. (For more information, see Chapter 6.)

ANNUAL REPORTS

This is the most lucrative market for corporate photographers. It is a demanding, exciting, and challenging field. It is also the toughest to break into.

What they do

Corporations are required by law to issue a financial report to stockholders once a year. This report has evolved from a detailed financial statement into a document that represents the company to investors, to other companies, and to the public. Corporations want the annual report to reflect an image of prosperity and quality. This is usually accomplished through design and photography.

Since so much rides on the annual report (it is, for an entire year, the face the corporation presents to the world), very few chances are taken. This means that any photographer going after major corporate annual reports must have a track record with other major corporate annual reports. Sound like a catch-22? It is.

Best bets

You can only break in through other routes. We know of one photographer whose press release picture of the Chairman of the Board so impressed the man that he would hear of no one else's photographing him for the annual report. The photographer had been calling on the studio handling the report for eight years without success. A nod from the top was the break he needed. The moral: Any shot can be the opportunity or make the contact to get the work you want.

Chances are that the first annual report you land will be for a small company with a limited budget. In the long run, the money for this particular job is not important. What matters is that you get terrific samples. Work with the designer and the printer, if you can, to make sure the report looks as good as possible. Remember that a mediocre printing job will make even great photographs look mediocre.

Who buys photography?

Usually one person at the corporation has overall responsibility for the annual report. That person will hire a design studio or advertising agency to design and produce the report, and either (or both) are then potential buyers of photography. Call the headquarters of the corporation and ask for the editor of the annual report. (For design studios, refer to the earlier section in this chapter.)

Inner workings

One practical note: The annual-report business is cyclical. The best time to make appointments is right after the report has been issued, sometime in late spring; the photography is usually done in the fall. The worst time to see anyone involved in annual-report work is during the final agony of production. This period usually starts in January and continues through April.

CORPORATE PUBLIC RELATIONS

An in-house public relations department operates much the same as the public relations agencies described earlier. In addition, it will handle newsletters (a large corporation produces many), slide presentations, and a grab bag of other sorts of communication.

A public relations department is an excellent way for a beginning photographer to start working with a corporation. Like the agencies, P.R. departments need high-volume, fast-turnaround, low-budget photography.

BREAKING IN . . . Joe Baraban

Joe Baraban is an award-winning Houston photographer doing national ads for clients around the country. He is also president of the Art Directors Club of Houston.

Even though I'm based [in] Houston, I'd say at least 60 percent to 70 percent of my work comes from other places. I picked Houston because, back in 1969, it was a fast-growing city, had a good atmosphere, and my sister already lived there—so I figured, if I ever needed a meal . . .

Houston turned out to be pretty good, because I kind of grew as the business out here grew. Houston and Dallas are a really big graphic-arts market. There're people here that are as good as anybody in the world.

To get anywhere, no matter what area you work out of, you have to have a lot of drive and a lot of ambition. Not blind ambition by any means, but just knowing what you want. I've had a direction, I've known where I was going for a long time. The day I put a camera in my hand I knew this was it.

So I started out by doing any job I could get; you just shoot everything you can. They ask you if you can do this and you say of course you can, even though you've never done it before. You can't say No; if you say No, they might not give you another chance. So you say Yes—and then go out and learn it.

One of the big obstacles when I was starting out was my age. I was 22 or 23, and people have a hard time trusting someone that young with a major job. And it was really tough convincing them to give you the work. But I had a lot of nerve and I'd just tell them that I could do it. Give me a chance, and if you don't like it you don't have to pay for it. It worked. And everybody liked the work. I've always believed that all they can do is say No. I'll ask anything. You've got nothing to lose.

I never just stop at one picture. I shoot a lot of film. I shoot a lot of pictures, and I'll do just about anything to get the shot. I never have any trouble finding a shot. It's always in front of you, you just have to piece it all together. When I walk into a shoot I never see what I want. I never photograph what I see: I photograph what I want to see. That's the way my style has evolved. That's pretty much the way I shoot. I set it up, make up the shot, and then shoot it reportage [style]. Coming from an art background, and then having worked for the wire services, the photojournalism and the art background have worked together to develop my style.

If you're planning to work as an advertising photographer, you should get as varied a background as possible. When I'm talking to my apprentices or to students, I can't tell them enough about the importance of design and art—and color. That is as important as any photography course you could take.

I think it's also important to . . . [be able to] talk on different levels with people. Being a great photographer is not all of it. You have to be able to communicate on some level other than "What camera do you use?" and "What film do you use?"

Then, to get started in the business, find a job working for a good photographer as an assistant. You need to learn the business; you need to learn photography. There's no way I know that you can get on top without starting on the bottom of it. It's a real cliché, but it's real, real true in this business. Three of the top shooters in this area were my assistants—real strong photographers.

The thing I look for when somebody comes to me looking for a job is their portfolio, and I don't care what the subject matter is. I don't care what they shoot. What I want to know is how professional that portfolio is. That portfolio better look like they know what they're doing. So many guys come in, and every photo is mounted on a different color background and it's different sizes. It's unprofessional, and I would never hire somebody like that. Or their prints aren't spotted or they're not neat. If they don't take care of their own work, they're not going to take care of mine. And I need that from them. They need to have respect for their own work.

CHAPTER 4

GETTING READY TO WORK

Not long ago there just wasn't much around in the way of photographic education. You really had to fend for yourself for the most part. Of course there were two or three schools, and some courses you could get through the mail, but that was about it. Most photographers either learned from reading magazines and ruining film or they got a job in the local studio or hung out at the newspaper office until somebody paid attention to them.

You can still do it that way if you want to, but things have changed. By now hundreds of schools across the country offer photography classes of some kind, and 75 of them offer four-year degrees. There are all sorts of workshops, taught by big-name people or local pros and covering almost every kind of work, taking place everywhere from Monterey to Moscow. There are two-year professional certificate programs. And at least one school working directly with an ad agency and one correspondence school will still tell you how to do it through the mail. When you get through with all of that, you can get a job as an assistant and work your way up from the bottom. All you have to do is supply the talent and the commitment.

It is possible to become a professional photographer without a formal photo education. Many of the most famous did it that way. The only thing is, most of them did it a long time ago, when there wasn't as much competition as there is now. Your competition has been to school. To keep up with them, you are going to need a photography-school education. It will not solve all your professional problems, but it will give you solid grounding in the basics of technique and vision, so that you can solve them for yourself.

This doesn't mean photography school is the only route. In fact, without a broad base of study in other fields you will not have much to say with your perfectly honed techniques. Without an artist's understanding of form, texture, color, and design, your pictures will be academic exercises. There is a balance in a good education, and this will give you an understanding of substance as well as technique. Quite a few students at the more specialized photography schools already have degrees in the arts or humanities or sciences. They see photography as a way to put that knowledge to use.

To put it another way: you have to be able to talk about something besides *f*-stops. In this business, you deal with a lot of people. You have to be able to communicate with them in order to do your job. For the most part, the buyers you approach when you're looking for work will not be photographers. They will be designers, commercial artists, engineers, writers, architects, doctors, lawyers, and the man in the street. The more you are able to understand them and what they do, the better your work will be.

Can you go into business or get a job right out of school? Well, no and yes. You can get a job. You can also go into business—but you probably wouldn't last long. There's a lot more to making a living in photography than can be learned in school. Most graduates will start out in a staff job of some kind. One of the best possible ways to start is as an assistant to a photographer whose work you admire. Your education will give you enough knowledge to begin learning from the real world. In fact, just about everybody we talked to, buyers and photographers alike, said that the best way to learn is to assist.

SCHOOLS

Let's take a look at some of the possibilities:

Colleges and Universities. The territory of the four-year degree, B.A. or B.S., these institutions offer the broadest choice of courses of study. A college degree is almost a necessity for photojournalism, absolutely necessary for medical or scientific work. It is possible to major in a different field while learning enough photography to get you started. A good college education will at least teach you to do research, an indispensable skill.

Except for some staff or scientific jobs, however, buyers want to see your pictures, not your degree.

Specialized Schools. Here we include art and design schools along with photography institutions. These are sometimes four-year programs but more often two or three. They generally give Bachelor of Fine Arts degrees for four years and Associate in Arts degrees or certificates for shorter courses. There is a vast range of type and quality of program: Most are quite specialized, but some offer a certain amount of study besides just art and photography. Check carefully to be sure your kind of work is among a school's strong points. Such a place can be a good choice for people who already have an academic degree and want to go into photography as a business.

A graduate of the Art Center School in Pasadena, California, Lynn Sugarman, had this to say about the experience:

> The program at the Art Center is really regimented. All along, it's geared toward creating a portfolio. When you leave there, I'd say your portfolio is probably the best of all the schools.
>
> They said the best photo student for Art Center was someone who didn't know photography that well, because then they could teach you the Art Center way of photography. The facilities there were wonderful. They had two huge stages, which broke down to about 15 or 20 spaces per stage that people could use. There was an equipment room where you could sign out strobes and things. You had to have your own cameras, though. You had to [have] 4 × 5, 2¼, and 35 mm [formats] before you even walked through the doors for your first semester. We had to turn in five to six assignments a week. It is very commercially oriented. There is very little of anything else.
>
> You did have to satisfy some liberal-arts requirements, I think; but, since I had a degree already, that didn't apply to me. Most of the students were right out of high school, and it was a real culture shock to all of a sudden have your life taken over by a school. I know it helped me to have a degree from another school, to come in a little older than most of the other students. It's really emotionally draining. And it's expensive, with tuition and materials costs. A lot of people would take a semester off to rest and make some money.
>
> Art Center doesn't have a placement program in photography; so you have to go out on your own and survey the market.

I think in Los Angeles the photographers are a little jaded because they see so many Art Center books. But in New York, if you take your book around to photographers for assistant work a lot of them say, "You should be out shooting"; but you know that you need the basic business sense that you can only learn from assisting.

Correspondence Schools. As far as we can tell, there is only one correspondence school left, the New York Institute of Photography. It offers a pretty good basic-to-intermediate photography course. The problem is that you are out there on your own in terms of actually doing the assignments. It takes a lot of motivation to get through a long photo course without a class group or instructor. The institution helps the student a lot by providing taped lectures coordinated with the printed texts and having assignments critiqued individually on tape by an instructor. The material they present is thorough and correct, if a little dated. All in all, if you can't do it any other way you can still learn photography through the mail.

Workshops. Perhaps the most recent option in photographic education is the workshop. There now seem to be an endless variety of workshops listed in the back of *American Photographer* and the other photo magazines, or promoted by various organizations and manufacturers. While you can't get a full basic photo education from any one of them, you could probably piece together something really fantastic. It would be expensive and would take you a lot longer than four years, but it's an interesting thought anyway.

Most workshops are aimed at intermediate-to-advanced photographers who are interested in a particular type of photography, in working with a certain (usually well-known) photographer or expert, in learning more about a specific manufacturer's equipment, or in traveling with a group of other photographers. The good ones offer access to people or to information usually out of reach to the public. They last anywhere from a weekend to two or three weeks, and prices vary according to length, accommodations, and a variety of other factors.

To find out about workshops, look in the photo magazines and in the newsletters or other publications of photographers' organizations such as the Professional Photographers of America or the American Society of Magazine Photographers.

Regardless of which options you choose, spend some time evaluating the different schools. Each has its own philosophy and teaching methods. Most are strong in certain areas but virtually ignore others. Check out the faculty. Sometimes a great teacher can do more for you than four years spent acquiring flawless technique. Talk to some students and recent graduates to find out what really goes on at the school. Find out what kinds of jobs recent graduates of that institution have gotten (the placement office will have this information). It's a big decision—take it seriously.

ASSISTING

Whether or not you study photography formally, there is absolutely no substitute for the experience of assisting. The system of an assistant's working for and learning from working professional photographers seems to be an informal version of the medieval apprentice system. In those days, the craft guilds administered one's progression from apprentice (student, then assistant) to journeyman (chief assistant, then the craftsman just out on his own) to master (which speaks for itself). Unlike the guild system, today there are no formal tests to move you on to the next plateau. It takes guts and the ability to do the work. Not every assistant will make it to working photographer, and not every photographer will be acknowledged as a master. It is good to remember, however, that Hiro began his career assisting Avedon, and even Avedon had to learn somewhere.

Photographers in every specialty use assistants. Those working for the higher rates in advertising or fashion photography will probably use at least one assistant on every shoot. In fields such as photojournalism they are used less often but in a large marketplace you should be able to find work assisting in almost any specialty.

What is an assistant, anyway? At the very lowest level, an assistant is simply a go-fer—somebody who runs errands, cleans up, and generally does what nobody else wants to do. Miserable job, right? Maybe, but in between being a go-fer you observe everything that goes on in the studio or on location: As you watch, you learn. Pretty soon you have learned enough to actually touch a piece of equipment. Maybe they'll let you load film. Maybe you'll spend a month or two in the darkroom processing film or printing. All this time you watch and you learn. You have endured years of school so that you can understand what you are seeing now. After a while they let you out of the darkroom and you might get to be second assistant on a shoot.

Once you get to be second assistant, you are at last right there at the camera during the shoot. This is where your real-world education will begin in earnest. All the tricks of the trade are in use here, and you will help out with them and learn them yourself. Work with even one photographer for a while in this capacity and you will be amazed at how much you can learn in a short period of time.

At a certain point—only you will know when—you will have reached a level of experience and confidence where you will be ready to take the next step. That step could be a promotion to first assistant to the person for whom you are already working. Some photographers have started in the darkroom and progressed through the ranks to studio manager, a position where they are solely responsible for the studio's day-to-day operations and may actually do an entire shoot. Clients come to know this person as reliable and competent, something an unknown photographer must prove before getting work from them. This process could easily span 10 years. The contacts built by the assistant during this time will be the base on which a career is built.

The major disadvantage to this apprenticeship method is the exposure to the style and techniques of only one photographer. It is very difficult to develop your own unique style, or look, when you have been thinking as much like your employer as possible for such a long time.

Moving up

The next step could be to freelance assisting. Every situation is unique, of course, but we would recommend freelancing. It can expose you to the style and working methods of many photographers, and the more you learn the better off you are. In fact, we feel it is a good idea to work for photographers in a variety of specialties. Often techniques usually known only to still-life specialists, for example, will come in handy for a location industrial shot; or something learned from an illustration job will also work for fashion. Experience in several fields is always useful. You may also discover a liking for a specialty you never considered before. You never know!

Freelance assisting is also a sort of dry run for freelance assignment photography. Many of the problems and solutions associated with getting work as an assistant are similar to those of getting work as a photographer: You must research the market, decide whom to call, make the calls, show your portfolio, follow up on the calls, and deal with constant rejection. Learning that this rejection is not personal, and working with it as a condition of doing business, is one of the most important lessons you can learn.

There is one major difference besides length of experience between a photographer and an assistant: rates. We will discuss photographers' rates later, but for now you should be aware of the ugly truth—you can't get rich as an assistant. In fact, you'll be doing well if you can get by. In New York, as of 1984, a full-time beginning assistant can expect to make about $100 to $150 per week. A freelance assistant will usually earn $40 to $75 per day, depending on experience, whereas the so-called "superassistants" can get as much as $100 per day or more. On the other hand, you are being paid for getting the best photographic education there is, with buyer contacts thrown in. That's hard to beat. So hard, in fact, that the A.S.M.P., American Society of Magazine Photographers, estimates that there are as many as 3,000 assistants working in New York alone.

The A.S.M.P. was one of the first organizations to recognize the special problems and needs of assistants. Chad Weckler, the former chairman of their assistants committee, has been working as an assistant in New York for eight years. He described the experience this way:

> I came to New York very cold. I had a few friends here, but that's about it. I think my dad, who is also a professional photographer, was right when he said, "It shouldn't be too easy for you if you really want to learn it from deep inside, from the very core, and have it stay there." I think they say, "No pain, no gain." It hurt.
>
> I had, coming into New York, a photographic education and a pretty darn good one, from Brooks Institute of Photography [in California]. It brought me right to zero. You have to imagine that, whatever you know now, it isn't nearly enough.
>
> As soon as I hit New York I started doing what every person must do if you want to assist. Everybody has exactly the same method of looking for work. You pick up the *American Showcase*, you pick up the *Creative Black Book*. Now there are even more books you can use. The advantage of these over the phone book is the pictures. They really tell you who the photographer is. If you know the kind of person you are, you can find someone you want to work with. You might look at some pictures and say, "Oooh, boring." You

might look at some others and say, "*Oooh*, exciting, who is that photographer?" Right there you have the address and phone number. You have to do some research. You have to start calling photographers. The best way to start is to be a freelancer looking for a steady job.

Remember that every assistant made that very first cold phone call. If somebody is working and you're not, they made more calls than you did. There's nothing difficult about looking for work. You just may have to make twenty phone calls before you get through to someone who can hire you.

Your first job, or any job at this point, can make or break your attitude toward your future career. It can be frustrating. If some of your first experiences are bad experiences, that can be enough to break you—and maybe that's good. Maybe you need to experience life a little bit more, toughen up your skin and then come back. Because that's the business; it's not easy, it's not meant to be easy, and it's very competitive. But a good assistant knows why he or she is there; they know there is a pot of gold at the end of the rainbow.

That's one of the good things about assisting. It allows you a foot into the door of professional photography without making a large financial commitment and losing a tremendous amount of face if you fail.

You're really an apprentice until you start to freelance. Then you're in business for yourself; like a professional photographer, you're a professional assistant.

In the first three years of assisting, you learn very quickly... When you leave school you forget [all that information] almost as fast as you learned it. After about three years of assisting, it becomes second nature.

Some people say that carrying all the equipment is the worst part of photography. It's kind of true, but it sort of brings you back to a working mentality. It's fun, but it's work, too.

In the eight years I've been assisting, I've assisted photographers in every field. I not only know lighting now, but also I can work in any photographic environment, whether it's studio or location. I can think right along with them and anticipate things that will come up.

BREAKING IN... Bonnie West

Bonnie West is a New York fashion photographer who has been in business about six years. She works with major magazines and advertising accounts.

When I went to Parsons they didn't have a photography department as they do now. I had to take as much graphic design as photography, so that I could go out and become an art director. It's great when an art director comes in here with a layout and I know all the language and can talk to them in their own terms. My degree is in Communication Design, with a concentration in photography.

I started assisting in school. My last semester I went through the apprenticeship program. My first choice was Irving Penn, but that didn't work out. The next person on my list was Barbara Walz, who was doing fashion and portraiture—which was just what I wanted to do. I worked for her for the three months of the last semester, and then she hired me after graduation.

I worked for Barbara Walz full-time. She was doing a book at the time, called *Fashion Makers*. The writer was the fashion editor of *The New York Times*. I assisted her in both shooting the photographs of the fashion designers on Seventh Avenue and printing them for publication, as well as in all her other work.

About this time I really lucked out. In 1978 all the newspapers in New York went on strike. Some of the editors from the major papers got together, rented an office, and started to put out their own paper, called *The City News*, which lasted for the two or three months they were on strike. They needed a photographer, and the *Times*'s fashion editor called me. I was still working for Barbara at the time, but she let me go out and shoot. I got paid $25 a story no matter how many pictures ran.

One of the stories we shot was on Geoffrey Beene. A little later he called me and he wanted pictures. The same thing happened with the top ten designers, and all of a sudden I had a business. From that day on I stopped assisting and started working as a photographer.

When the newspapers came back on, I wasn't union or staff so I couldn't work for the *Times*. [But the fashion editor] introduced me to the fashion editor at the *Times*'s

Sunday magazine, which is totally [separate] from the [daily] newspaper. She started using me to shoot the New York fashion shows, and that's how it really started. I kind of fell into it.

It just snowballed. Once people start seeing tear sheets and seeing your work in the magazine, they automatically think you're a professional—you're delivering a job and you're getting paid well for your work. With those tear sheets I was developing a portfolio. A lot of the P.R. firms that were using me had advertising departments; so I started getting things from them. A year and a half later I was able to rent this studio. They gave me a chance—it worked out. After that, it's who you know.

Through the editor from the *Times,* I got names of more major P.R. firms with fashion accounts. I started by seeing them. For example, one worked with a shoe manufacturer. They called and said, "Could you do a pair of shoes for us? We're doing an article in a Miami newspaper." They sent over a pair of shoes, and on the dining room table in my apartment, with some seamless paper and one hot light, I shot the picture. It came out fine. The next day the woman calls me: "We have twenty more pairs, can you do them for a press kit?" I didn't even know what to bill them, but there I was with twenty pairs of shoes. I called some people to figure out a price. The client liked everything, and I still work for them.

I stopped doing the shows for the *Times Magazine* after five years. It was enough. I had gotten what I needed out of it. Now I'll go up there and show them my new work to let them know I can do other things and try to get them to take me that step further.

Some magazines will give me assignments that have nothing to do with what I show them. I went to *Gentleman's Quarterly* with my portfolio of fashion, still life, and portraiture—so they called me to do two interiors of stores in Georgetown. That's not really want I want to do; but when you get a story from *GQ* you want to prove yourself. I'll keep calling them. It will just take time.

I think fashion photography, like any other industry, is very trendy and it goes through cycles. Right now, it seems that the trend seems to be a lot of hot lights, a lot of shadows, very "artsy." My work is conservative. It emulates Avedon, Irving Penn . . . the light is really clean and my photographs are very graphically planned out. I don't think that's selling as well now as the hot light, real grainy look. That's not what I do. It's not what I like. I think when the trend goes back to the clean, sharp image, I'll be far more successful.

You can't just let it be, you have to make it work. It takes a long time to learn how to see: to visualize and be able to see what you want on film. I would say the best way to learn is to assist. What I learned with Barbara was her rapport between herself and the client and herself and the subject. And I could have used more of that. Go out there and assist as many people as you can and really learn the business.

I feel I'm on the right road. It's been six years, and you've got to have a lot of patience. I honestly feel I haven't wasted any time. Once I signed the lease to the studio, it was a dedication. Work came first—before friendships, relationships, anything.

CHAPTER 5

EQUIPMENT AND SERVICES

We cannot develop and print a memory.
—HENRI CARTIER-BRESSON

Every photographer must have some means of actually making a picture appear: Equipment is a necessary evil. "Evil" because it is so seductive and so much fun to look at, buy, play with, and collect that it's easy to forget that a camera or a light is only a tool. Don't get me wrong, you shouldn't be indifferent to equipment. It is, after your own skill and vision, the most important thing you have to work with.

You should know as much as you can about cameras, lenses, lights, etc., in order to use their full potential to your advantage. But don't let the machine control the man. There is the ever-present danger of becoming so involved with the "toys" and the technology that we lose sight of the main idea: the pictures we started out to create. This advice comes to you from a reformed equipment junkie.

BUY THE BEST, NOT THE MOST

Start by analyzing the jobs that are most likely to come up in the immediate future, say the next year or so. Make sure you have the basic equipment (camera bodies, lenses, lights, accessories) to do these jobs. Don't get carried away and decide you need the entire Nikon system before you can possibly call yourself a professional.

A fashion photographer we know began her career with a Nikormat, a 50mm lens, and some used electronic flash units. Five years later, after being regularly published in *Vogue, Brides,* and other magazines, she decided she needed more equipment. She bought one new 105mm lens.

You really don't need much to make great pictures.

There are so many brands of equipment on the market and so many models in so many price categories that even equipment junkies get confused. Some manufacturers' claims for their products seem too good to be true. And many of them are. Remember that the camera and lighting systems you choose now are going to be with you for a long time: Select for quality first and price second.

Professional photography demands much more of your equipment than snapshots do. Lenses must be sharp and free from optical flaws and must render accurate, rich, fully saturated color. Camera bodies and lighting systems should be simple and durable. You can't afford to have equipment break down in the middle of a job.

This doesn't necessarily mean buying only top-of-the-line (and therefore pricey) equipment. There are some good buys in most manufacturers' bottom-line camera bodies, and this is a good way to start building a professional system at minimal cost. As you need more technical options, you can keep the lenses and most of the accessories and invest in more versatile camera bodies.

The same holds true for lighting systems. Buy the best equipment appropriate to your specialty that you can afford at the time, with an eye toward expanding as business warrants it.

Support equipment such as tripods and even bags should also be of the highest quality you can afford. There's no getting around it: You get what you pay for.

CONSIDER USED EQUIPMENT

Equipment dealers and camera stores may sell used equipment taken in trade or bought outright, and some very high quality used equipment turns up in want ads in local papers. But consider it carefully. If you buy from a dealer, make sure he stands behind the equipment with at least a 30-day guarantee. If you buy from a source other than a reputable dealer, you are on your own.

It's possible to find excellent bargains in camera, lighting, and darkroom equipment offered by private individuals. The deals to stay away from are those where the equipment needs repair or is overpriced. Buy only the most expensive kinds of equipment secondhand. Cheaper items can easily be bought new, with the advantage of full guarantees. As a rule of thumb, buy used equipment from amateur photographers—they're easier on it. Professionals tend to use hardware until it's on its last legs.

When checking out used equipment, do the following:

1. Look the item over carefully. Any serious scratches, dents, or other exterior signs of wear or heavy use should make you think twice. Make sure all the seams still meet in the right places and that everything fits. If it looks badly worn, it probably is.
2. If it is a view camera, try out all the controls. Make sure all the locks still lock: Some worn cameras have a tendency to slip after adjustments are made.
3. Open the camera body and look inside: Is anything worn, broken, or just "not right"? Fire the shutter a few times, watching it from both front and back. If it is an SLR, pay special attention to the mirror.
4. Hold the camera body next to your ear and fire the shutter, trying each shutter speed in succession. Can you hear a difference in each speed? Also listen for any unusual grinding or crunching noises in the gear train during slow speeds.
5. If you are buying a lens, check the focusing mount and the aperture ring: They should be smooth and relatively tight, not loose and sloppy. If it is a large-format lens mounted in a shutter, use the same checks as above.
6. Open the lens and look through it. Check out both front and back elements for scratches, dents, and missing chunks.

These are the basics of checking out cameras and lenses, but the principle of examining equipment methodically is the same for anything. If you have any doubts when you think you've found a good deal, have the item checked out by a repairman who is familiar with the brand and type.

Last, but maybe most important, make sure whatever it is

really belongs to the seller. Hot equipment may be cheap, but it's really not a good idea to encourage theft. How would you feel if it was *your* recently stolen Hasselblad being sold for $100? Think about it.

Rent it if you don't have it

Some equipment is so specialized it's simply not worth owning for the one or two jobs a year that might need it. Fortunately, specialized equipment is available for rent in most major cities.

For example: You've just picked up an assignment for some new clients and think an 8mm fish-eye lens would deliver just the visual impact they're looking for. Don't try to make do with your 24mm, because it won't work. And don't spend the $700 for something you won't use again for a year. Instead, rent the 8mm from the nearest store with a rental service or one of the mail-order rental organizations who advertise in the back pages of the trade magazines. If you are far from a large city you will have to figure shipping costs and time into the rental fees.

In all cases, be sure that there is enough money in the job to justify the extra expense or that you can bill the rental cost. (More on how to estimate and bill a job in Chapter 9.)

Occasionally, being only human, you may keep rental equipment longer than you thought you would. So long, in fact, that the rent approaches or exceeds the purchase price. Most dealers will recognize this dilemma, and will either cut the rental price or allow you to apply what you would have paid in rent to purchase of the equipment.

This really works to your advantage if you are able to bill the rental costs to the job. The job can help you buy some new equipment—but don't explain it to the client this way. (They hardly ever understand!)

SEARCH BEFORE YOU BUY

Always consider your needs first, then what is available, and then comparative prices. Read the ads and equipment reviews in various magazines, or examine manufacturers' literature you can get from your dealer or direct by mail. An excellent source of information on large-format camera equipment, darkroom equipment, and many other photographic items is the Calumet Catalog. It's available by writing to Calumet at 890 Supreme Drive, Bensenville, Illinois, 60106.

Read between the lines in all cases, though. The magazines try to keep their advertisers happy; so they tend to dwell on the strong points of any equipment they test. You usually have to read very carefully to discover the full story.

Be sure you know the real price, not the list price, of any item *before* you go out, checkbook in hand, to buy it. The ads in the back of *Popular Photography* or *Modern Photography* are the best source for the lowest possible prices in the United States. Sometimes it's a lower price than your dealer pays for the same item. But compare these prices to those of your local supplier and, if the difference is no more than 10-to-15 percent, consider buying from him. If it's much more, show your dealer the printed price you have found and see how close he can come to it. If he can't come close, consider either going to one of the discount stores yourself or ordering from them by mail.

Here's an example: Suppose you decide you need a longer lens. The 135mm you have now just doesn't have the reach you need to get the football players' expressions during a tackle. About twice the image size would be adequate; so you decide you need a 300mm. So much for your basic needs. Now, Nikon offers three different 300mm lenses. One is very fast—$f/2.8$. It is also very expensive (in the vicinity of $2,000) and very large and heavy. You decide against this one right away on the grounds that limited use would not justify the price, and besides, with today's fast films you could get by with one of the slower versions. This leaves you with two 300mm $f/4.5$ lenses. One is a state-of-the-art lens, relatively small and light, made with Nikon's best glass and having internal focusing but costing $600—less than the first but twice as much as the third lens, the other of the same speed. This last one is an older design, slightly heavier but still very good, and a good buy at $300. Your choice? The best you can afford.

If at all possible, this means the middle lens; in this case, the $600 300mm $f/4.5$ lens. There may only be a small difference in performance between these second two, but it might be enough to give your pictures the edge they need. Also, you have a lens that probably will not be replaced in the near future by one that's twice as fast and half the price. In short, you've gotten the most for your money. And you can always rent that expensive $f/2.8$ if you really need it.

Build a relationship with a dealer

A good relationship with a local photo dealer has many advantages. The owner will probably stock the brands and quantities of supplies you use regularly if he knows he can count on you as a regular customer. He may be willing to help you find used equipment, take some of yours in trade, and provide you with "loaners" or rental equipment. A friendly dealer can be invaluable when you need to open a charge account or want some quick technical advice. His prices will usually be higher than those of the discount stores, but you're paying for personal attention and service impossible to get otherwise.

WHAT DO YOU REALLY NEED?

The lists that follow include some basic equipment for different formats. These lists are to be used only as guides. They are designed to give you an idea of the very minimum of camera-related equipment necessary to do most jobs. Of course there will be variations dictated by specialty; some of these are given in another list in the table of specialties (see pages 18–25). We do not suggest that you should limit yourself to what we mention here. Your own work habits and jobs will determine what you actually need.

Go shopping for lights

We will not consider lighting equipment here. The choice is so great, and so dependent on the individual style of the photographer, that it would be impossible even to list the possibilities. It's worth mentioning, however, that electronic flash units (often miscalled *strobes*) have become the light source of choice for most professionals. They are available in tiny, automatic, camera-mounted versions called *speedlights*, in powerful but compact portable units able to work with several heads (two or more lamps plugged into a single power generator), and monster studio setups sometimes brighter than the sun. Incandescent (or tungsten) sources, also known as "hot lights" for obvious reasons, are still used by some photographers, mostly for tabletop still lifes and interiors.

BASIC EQUIPMENT OUTFITS BY FORMAT

SMALL FORMAT (35mm)

Camera bodies (1 or 2, with built-in exposure meters)

Wide-angle 24mm f/2.8 lens

Standard 50mm f/1.4 lens

Short telephoto 135mm f/2.8 lens

Heavy-duty bag for above

Tripod

MEDIUM FORMAT

6cm × 6cm (2¼-inch-square), 6cm × 7cm, 6cm × 4.5cm

Camera bodies (1 or 2)

Extra roll film back or insert

Camera back for Polaroid Land film

Hand-held exposure meter/flash meter

Moderate-wide-angle lens (50mm for 6 × 6 cm format)

Standard lens (80mm for 6 × 6cm)

Medium-long lens (150mm for 6 × 6 cm)

Tripod

VIEW CAMERAS, LARGE FORMAT (4 × 5 in., 8 × 10 in.)

Camera body

Film holders

Polaroid Land film holder

Hand-held exposure meter/flash meter

Dark focusing cloth

Loupe

Cable release

Standard lens (180mm or 210mm for 4 × 5 cm format)

Heavy-duty tripod

Processing lab

The most important service you will use as a photographer is the processing lab. Nothing is more damaging to your reputation and your business than to have an entire day's shooting ruined in the lab. How do you minimize this risk? By knowing as much as you can about the lab you're planning to use. In the case of wedding and portrait photographers, this may be a mail-order operation specializing in your business. For the in-house industrial photographer, it is probably a processing lab in the same department. But for the freelancer, photojournalist, or other independent worker, it is usually Eastman Kodak for Kodachrome, the local custom lab for all other color, and your own darkroom for black and white. Whatever your situation, make sure you are working with the most reliable people.

A relatively small number of labs serve only (or primarily) professional clients, but in most cities and towns there will be at least one. It is to your advantage to use one of these labs, for the simple reason that you will get good, consistent results and service. There is no need to feel intimidated, no matter what your current level of photography. In fact, some of these labs offer discounts and other specials to the assistants of photographers who use their service: The assistants of today are the big clients of tomorrow.

Ask around. Find out which lab the top photographers in your area use, and check it out. Better to spend a litte more money and get a good consistent product than cut corners and lose a job.

Equipment repair

Everything breaks. If you use it a lot, it breaks more often. The demands of professional photography are as great on the equipment as they are on the photographer, and a camera body that might last the average amateur a lifetime can be turned into a worn-out paperweight by a busy pro in just a few years. A pro may shoot miles of film in a day, and risks like cold, frequent air travel, salt sea spray, and just plain banging around also increase the need for access to good repair people.

So, even if it doesn't die entirely, your equipment will need a little cleaning and tune-up now and again. A good repair service, one that knows your brand and type of equipment, is essential. In major cities it's fairly easy to get service on major brands—Leica, Nikon, Canon, Hassleblad, Linhof, etc. In remote areas, you may have to send the item off to the next large town or even back to the manufacturer. Once again, the best way to find good, reliable service is to ask other photographers. They will gladly tell you who knows what they are doing and who to stay away from. If you have something a little exotic for your area and nobody knows who works on it, write or telephone the manufacturers. They will usually send you a list of authorized repair shops. If you travel a lot, it's a good idea to take along such a list in case something goes wrong in a strange city or country.

Other services

Besides lab and repair people, here are some other places you will want to list in your card file.

Hardware store. No matter what kind of work you do, you will probably find yourself in need of all kinds of strange hardware items. From tools to clamps to the indispensable gaffers' tape and other things too numerous to mention, a well-stocked, knowledgeable hardware store can save the day. Get to know the people on the counter—their suggestions can be very helpful.

Art-supply store. Even if you aren't a weekend painter, you will probably use something from an art store. They stock or can order for you portfolios and mounting board, large white and silver cards you can use as reflectors, and drafting vellum—which is great light-diffusion material. Book departments in many art stores include photography annuals and design award books that will keep you in touch with what is going on in the business, as well as being terrific stimuli for your own picture ideas. There's more, but we don't want to spoil your fun.

Modeling agency or school. Whenever your specialty involves photographing people, you will occasionally need models. Of course, if you do fashion or illustration or things like that you will need them often. In a large market you can choose from several agencies, many of them specializing in certain types. Smaller markets may have some version of a modeling school that also functions as an agency. Models, like photographers, need portfolios ("books") in order to get work, and so when you want to shoot test pictures to build your portfolio, you can usually get models to pose in exchange for prints or duplicate transparencies.

This is a great arrangement, since both the photographer's and the model's work gets shown in the other's books.

Travel agent. Ever need tickets in a hurry on a flight the airline said was full? Call your friendly travel agent; sometimes they can find a seat magically when you need it. If you need to organize rental cars, hotels, and other facilities in a faraway place, you can spend days of valuable time on the phone trying to set up the arrangements. Sometimes one call to the travel agent is all you need. There is usually no fee for their services because they collect from the other end.

Others. There are all sorts of other services you will need at one time or another; the best listing of them is your local Yellow Pages. The Yellow Pages is the definitive reference source for goods and services in your area. If you can't find what you need in there, you probably can't get it. Your phone company will provide you with both business and consumer versions for any city in the U.S.A. You might want to get copies from the surrounding communities, as well as those from some large cities. The New York City business-to-business version is useful no matter where you live.

BREAKING IN ... Ross Baughman

Ross Baughman is a photojournalist and head of Visions Photo Group. He won the Pulitzer Prize for his photographs of the revolt in Rhodesia.

Visions was originally a Camelot-type of fantasy—that I was going to be able to invite the best photographers I'd ever met to get together under one roof and become familiar with each others' work. We designed it as kind of a Ma-and-Pa agency, as opposed to the high-powered full-service mass-market European photo agencies [like] Sygma and Black Star and Magnum.

When they all started up, they depended on photographers who were willing to rush headlong into world events—the latest war, celebrity scandal—shooting at their own risk, with their own money, willing to rush back in with photographs and dump them on an editor's desk. We planned to concentrate on magazine essays that required a long time to shoot, that required a different kind of photography.

There are probably three photographers who have survived from the original group. I think the biggest problem photographers have when they want to join an agency is exaggerated expectations. They think the photo agent is going to procure assignments, pay their electricity bill when they're on the road, send lawyers, guns, and money when they find themselves in trouble. An agency can't do that.

We're paid day rates against the ultimate display that the magazine gives our photographs. If I went out one day and photographed a K.K.K. rally where I was lucky enough to stumble onto strong situations (lynchings, burnings, etc.), then there's a good chance the magazine might want to use a cover or five, six, or seven inside pages. If they do that, they've certainly gotten more than the $300 a day rate from me. They apply that—the $300 already promised—as a kind of down payment against [the fee due] when the magazine finally appears and they've racked up a space rate. At most magazines, a page is the equivalent of a day's rate. So they're going to have to give you $2100 more to make up the difference.

A good place for a young photographer to start is as a

stringer. I started that way, working my summers during high school and college shooting for the local newspaper. As a stringer, you're always up against the staffers for jobs. You get paid per picture. When you consider the caliber of photographers that are willing to work, for example, for a wire service in the beginning of their careers, making almost nothing, you realize that it's strictly for the access that they get to major news events.

I can remember working for the Associated Press and giving them pictures for five dollars apiece. They turn it around and sell it to thousands of newspapers and make a bundle. After about a year of that, I thought that I could be making a much better living for myself if I figured out how to break into the magazine field.

When you look at the tradition, the photographer has been looked at as the low person on the totem pole, the one who manages to go out there and be on time—the old expression was, "f/8 and be there!"—and come back with the shot. The tradition at newspapers and magazines used to be that they had to have a reporter along with them who more or less picked up their leash and gave it a tug.

Today, the average stringer is better educated, more highly motivated, more intelligent than that old stereotype. But there's still a great need for press photographers to think like reporters: to do more of the groundwork, to be more aware of the larger meaning of the story. They've got to be able to put it into context.

When you're just taking competent, clean, storytelling pictures, that only gets you in the door as a capable photographer. You have to make your reputation on delivering some zing, something really exciting. That's where the pressure falls squarely on the storyteller—the photojournalist—to come up with interesting, provocative, fresh views of the world.

CHAPTER 6

THE JOB

Patience, and shuffle the cards.

—MIGUEL DE CERVANTES

The bottom line for all photographers is the job. Its performance and delivery differ greatly from one specialty to another, but in the end it's the reason the business of photography exists at all. Once you've decided what kind of photo work you want to do, acquired the equipment, and mastered the techniques, you must actually go out there and put them to work. You're going to have to find a job, if you plan to be a staff photographer, or many jobs, if you're going to freelance.

The process for each of these is quite similar, so we're going to approach the subject of the job in four major sections: finding, getting, doing, and getting paid for the job.

Finding It

Having chosen a specialty and studied the market, you now need to find the specific company or agency you want to get work from, identify the person responsible for hiring photographers or buying photographic services, and contact them.

Getting It

Your objective is to convince the person you see that you are the person who will do the best possible job. Your portfolio is your most important tool. It should be directed at the specific market, organization, or publication, even the specific person who is going to see it.

Doing It

You'll only get one chance to do any job. The way to make sure you do it right is to make sure you understand what the client wants and what you need to do to create those pictures.

The job is only over when the client has accepted and paid for the finished photos. Make sure your post-production procedures are equal to your shooting performance. Above all, never promise more than you can deliver and *always meet your deadlines*.

Getting Paid for It

An important part of this process is agreeing on the budget *before you start shooting the pictures*—that is, if you are applying for a staff position, your salary and benefits; if you are a freelancer or a studio owner, what the client will pay for your services and reimburse for job-related expenses.

FINDING THE JOB: RESEARCHING YOUR MARKET

Good research is one of the things that separates those who work from those who don't. There is no substitute for being well informed about the business you plan to approach. The first in-depth research you will have to do concerns the organizations and people you want to work for or sell your services to. The following plan is designed for photographers who will be working in one of the commercial specialties.

STEP BY STEP

Step 1. Find a library with an extensive collection of periodicals and strong economics (yes, economics) and reference sections. If you are a college student, your university library will be just fine. If you aren't, use the largest public library in your community or have a friend introduce you at a college library.

Step 2. Get a notebook and a pen. Give yourself at least a half a day for preliminary research and head for the library. (If you get tired of the research, it's also a good place to meet people.)

Step 3. Start with the current-periodicals room. You have already chosen a specialty and have some idea what kind of work is being done in it. Now you are going to go into this in much more depth. Magazines are excellent places to see the work of professional advertising and editorial photographers and to get an understanding of what works in which specialty. Begin with the most popular magazines, the ones that are familiar to you. Look carefully at the pictures in all copies on hand—the checklist below may help.

Step 4 (but still the preliminary stage). Try to find other magazines that use the kind of photography you're interested in. Look for magazines you've never seen before, maybe foreign, limited-subscription, or trade publications. Be sure to include regional publications because they are among the best markets for beginners. Ask the librarian for help. Be as specific as you can about what you're looking for. If you spend a little time describing what you're doing, a good librarian can offer an astounding amount of help. For example, if you are interested in corporate work you will probably be sent to the economics section to look not only at the annual reports but also at various obscure guides and indexes.

Use the checklist as a guide while studying all these periodicals.

PERIODICALS PHOTO CHECKLIST

1. To which pictures do you respond positively? Which negatively? Why? (Consider lighting, subject, composition, color, treatment, etc.)
2. How are the pictures used? (Advertising, part of a story, single illustration? Large, small, double-page spread?) Does the style change with use?
3. Are they mostly color or black and white? Why one or the other?
4. What is the subject matter of these photographs and how is it handled?
5. How were they done? (Studio, location? Small camera, large format, view camera? Complex lighting, existing light? Sets, costumes, props?)
6. If credit is given, list the photographers whose work you liked.
7. If the photographs appear in ads, list the advertisers you think used the most effective pictures.

8. List the periodicals that consistently publish the pictures most interesting to you.

9. If the pictures are in some specialty other than advertising or editorial—scientific, portrait, wedding, for example—list the organizations or studios for which they were taken.

10. Go back over your lists and mark the photographers and organizations in your geographic area.

Step 5. Now you have a list of magazines that publish the kind of photographs that interest you. Fascinating, right? Isn't there a lot more going on out there than you thought? Pick some of your favorites from the list now and go through the back issues. It's useful to go back as far as the library's collection will let you: Start there, skip ahead a year or two and look at a couple of issues; continue this spot-checking up to the present.

Step 6. As you do this, continue to notice the names of photographers and also the advertisers or other organizations who commissioned pictures. This way, you'll get a short course in the history of your specialty. It's a good base to build your style on.

Step 7. That's enough for your first visit to the library. Go home and think about what you have seen. Take a look at your most recent pictures. Consider them in light of currently published work. Are you headed in the right direction? This is the easiest time to adjust your goals.

You now have a good idea of the current state of work in your specialty, as well as its recent history. You also have a list of the organizations or publications who paid for these pictures. This is your market. These (and others like them) are the buyers who will give you work.

If you plan to work as an assistant, approach the photographers whose work you admired. There's no better way to get started in the business than to work with an established professional with a good reputation.

Remember that the photographers whose work appears in the magazines have had much more experience than you. Don't expect to be Richard Avedon overnight, but don't let the high quality of those pictures intimidate you, either. Once you find out what you want and how to go about getting it, there's no reason it won't be *your* photographs in *Scientific American* or *Playboy* that some beginner will be studying a few years from now.

DIGGING DEEPER: DIRECTORIES

Take your lists and notebook and go back to the library. This time you're ready to get more specific about your market and you'll need some special reference books: You're going to leave the library with names and phone numbers of people who buy the kind of photography you want to do.

The books are listed by market type and you'll find them in either the reference or the economics section. Look for the ones appropriate to the market you're interested in. Again, a good librarian can be a great help and might know of regional or local directories that would be useful. (Since these are reference books, they probably may not leave the building; so you'll have to copy the information you need. Tedious, but necessary.)

A WORD OF CAUTION ABOUT DIRECTORIES

Many of these books will give specific names and telephone numbers of photo buyers. They were probably correct when the book went to press; but that was months ago—if not years. So don't panic if, when you call XYZ, Inc., and ask for George Smith, you find he doesn't work there anymore. Unless the company no longer uses photography, George has probably been replaced by someone. Ask who the replacement is and then talk to that person.

Advertising

Here is a short list of standard directories that will be useful.

Standard Directory of Advertising Agencies. *National Register Publishing Company. 5201 Old Orchard Road, Skokie, IL 60077.*

Known as "the Red Book," this is the definitive listing of ad agencies—more than three thousand of them. They are listed geographically and also by specialty. Information includes the agency's gross yearly billings and number of employees (so you can see how large an agency it is), the year founded, any specialization, and a client list. It also lists clients added since the last issue of the directory. The more new clients, the more new work—and opportunities.

Art directors, creative directors, and other key agency people are listed by name and title. If the agency has branch offices in other cities, the addresses and phone numbers appear, along with names of key people there.

Start with the geographical listings and look up agencies in your area. Check their clients and billings to find out the size of the agency and the kind of work they do.

Match up some of the ads you noticed during your investigation to the clients on the agency list. (Remember that a local agency probably doesn't create national ads for the large companies, and so a local agency that lists Pepsi-Cola as a client probably does advertising for a local bottling plant or a regional headquarters.) As you match ads with their agencies you will start to see styles. Typically, an art director's or agency's work will have a personality. It can be identified in the types and number of pictures used, the amount of copy (words) in an ad, a particular graphic (design) approach. Keep watching for any style characteristic that shows up consistently at any particular agency. Some of these styles will fit your talents better than others: Those are the ad agencies you should call first.

As another source, see the listing for the same publisher's *Standard Directory of Advertisers*. This is the companion volume to the Red Book. It lists, by business and industry, the companies that advertise and names their advertising agency or agencies.

Adweek Directory of Advertising (by year and region) *Adweek. 820 Second Avenue, New York, NY 10017.*

A terrific source. More concise than the Red Book because it's regional, it lists not only advertising agencies but also advertisers (by brand name), public relations agencies, and all major advertising media in that region. It names names and gives addresses and telephone numbers. It also has background articles. Where else would you get a listing of the ten hottest agencies of the previous year?

Audiovisual markets

Audiovisual Market Place. *R. R. Bowker Company. 1180 Avenue of the Americas, New York, NY 10036.*

This comprehensive listing of audiovisual producers and production companies includes the type of work each one does and provides some useful names. Not as complete as it could be, it's a good starting point. The Yellow Pages in your area might be a better bet for local A.V. studios. Look under either *Audiovisual* or *Graphic design* headings: Between them, you should be able to find just about all you need. Look for companies doing a lot of speech support and multimedia, training, or educational film-strips.

Corporate/industrial markets

Standard Directory of Advertisers. *National Register Company, Inc. 5201 Old Orchard Road, Skokie, IL 60077.*

This directory is extremely useful in unearthing corporate markets. It lists more than seven thousand companies by type of business and by location. The classification by business makes it much easier to figure out just what the XYZ Corporation does and whether it can use your kind of photography. The geographical listing tells you whether they're within striking distance.

Things to look for include names of advertising manager, creative director, art director, public relations manager, corporate communications manager, or any other title that sounds as if it has something to do with advertising or communications. Chances are you won't want to talk directly to the Vice President of Marketing, but you will want to telephone that department to find out who buys photography there.

If the company uses an advertising agency, it will be listed. If, instead, the listing reads *Direct*, the company handles whatever advertising and promotion they do in-house. This can mean a large department or it can mean one advertising manager who hires freelancers as needed. These are excellent places for a photographer to begin a career.

If nothing is listed under the *Advertising agency* heading and the company has only 50 employees, don't waste your time: Unless they're either next door to you or you know for a fact that they use photography, you'll spend more effort than it's worth.

O'Dwyer's Directory of Corporate Communications. *J.R. O'Dwyer Company, Inc. 271 Madison Avenue, New York, NY 10016.*

Similar to the *Standard Directory of Advertisers,* but much more focused, this annual publication lists more than two thou-sand companies and three hundred trade organizations, with names of their public relations executives. They are classified both geographically and by industry. Use it much the same as the *Standard Directory,* starting with companies in your area. In fact, if you're just interested in the public relations people at a company, this directory will be more useful: It gives you less information on the company itself, but pinpoints the appropriate people more directly.

Working Press of the Nation, Volume V: Internal Publications Directory. *National Research Bureau. 424 North Street, Burlington, IA 52601.*

This book lists thousands of company magazines, with the editors' names and addresses, broken down by industry and by circulation but not by geography. It's going to be a little harder to find the buyers in your area, but you might start by picking an industry and looking for local companies in that group.

You may not have found many company magazines as you looked through the periodicals shelved at your library, but this is a very good market. Corporations and other large organizations publish everything from newsletters to well designed, beautifully printed magazines. All of these require photography. Those published by large corporations, or having large circulations, pay very well. They will also give you good exposure and first-rate samples.

To get copies of the magazines that seem interesting, call or write to the company and ask for sample copies.

O'Dwyer's Directory of Public Relations Firms. *J. R. O'Dwyer Company, Inc. 271 Madison Avenue, New York, NY 10016.*

This guide lists nearly a thousand public relations businesses, dividing them both geographically and by specialty. The methods of use outlined above for similar guides also apply here.

MacRae's State Industrial Directories. *MacRae's Blue Book, Inc. 817 Broadway, New York, NY 10003.*

A separate directory issued yearly for each state, these list (as far as we can tell) every company and business in the state, size no object. For example, the same section of the Connecticut directory lists both Xerox Corporation headquarters and a place called Vac-U-Form (5 employees). Giving essentially the same information as the *Standard Directory of Advertisers*, it also classifies the companies by product. This means that, if you have a great idea for photographing tents and backpacks, you can find out who manufactures them in your state and see if they're interested.

Inc. *Inc. Publishing Corporation. 38 Commercial Wharf, Boston, MA 02110.*

Inc. calls itself "The magazine for growing companies" and, as such, it is a wonderful source for names of fast-growing new companies. Each year it publishes a top-500 list, a fastest-growing-100 list, and a most-successful-entrepreneur list. Many of the organizations on these lists will find themselves suddenly in need of all sorts of photography. If any are near you, it is definitely worthwhile to find out who buys their photography and make contact with that person.

Photojournalism

Gebbie Press All-In-One Directory. *Gebbie Press. Box 1000, New Paltz, NY 12561.*

Gebbie's is one of the most useful guides around. It not only lists more than seventy-five hundred newspapers, magazines, and other periodicals but also gives circulation figures and identifies "target" audiences. It also divides these publications into 200 categories, to make it easier to match your specialty to a publication. It has one major drawback: no phone numbers. You'll have to get those from the telephone book.

Business Publications. *Standard Rate and Data Service. 5201 Old Orchard Road, Skokie, IL 60077.*

This is the best listing of trade publications. It does not provide editors' names but does provide four thousand or so titles, addresses, and phone numbers of publications. Like *Gebbie*'s, it breaks down its listings into 159 categories, making it easier for you to identify your own market. It also lists circulation and advertising rates—which are useful indicators (see next entry).

Consumer Magazine and Farm Publications. *Standard Rate and Data Service. 5201 Old Orchard Road, Skokie, IL 60077.*

Similar to the company's *Business Publications*, this directory lists consumer magazines, which generally pay higher rates. Information includes circulation and advertising rates, as well as statements of general editorial policy. This book is the bible for advertising agencies when they are making up print-ad budgets. It is considered to be absolutely accurate. The publications with the highest ad rates will pay the most for photography. Those in the middle-to-low ranges will be your best bet as a new photographer. This directory uses only 51 categories to classify listings.

Ulrich's International Periodicals Directory. *R.R. Bowker Company. 1180 Avenue of the Americas, New York, NY 10036.*

Foreign periodicals, while they usually don't pay as well as

American ones, are nevertheless a very good market for American feature material. Photographers often sell the same story to magazines in different countries. This is completely legal. Foreign magazines have also been known to assign stories to photographers in the U.S.A. whose work they know. *Ulrich's* lists (are you ready for this?) about sixty thousand periodicals under one thousand specialty headings. Pay attention to the circulation figures here, and try the bigger ones first. Some of those listed are highly specialized and very small. Often the larger magazines have offices in New York, and so you can submit material to them in the United States rather than having to send it overseas. You might also telephone them and ask for sample copies, if the magazine is not available in your area.

Other markets

More sources (such as design annuals and advertising award books) are listed in the appendix. You may or may not want to use them to get work, but they're terrific sources for ideas and inspiration.

ONWARD AND UPWARD

When you finish with *this* library session you should have enough material to keep you occupied for at least a year. Say Goodbye and Thank You to the librarian, and go home to start the next step.

Properly used, the lists you have put together will get you your first job and start you out on your career.

Before you actually begin to contact people, though, you should spend a little more time with those lists. Let them age a day or two. Then go back over them and pick out the ten company names that seem both most interesting and nearest. Concentrate on these for your first campaign, as follows:

STEP BY STEP

Step 1. Check to make sure you have seen examples of the pictures used by all companies. If you haven't, try the library again (they'll remember you) or write to the concern directly asking for examples.

Step 2. Start a notebook or a file for each of these companies. If you can include actual examples of their publications or pictures, do so. If not, include notes on what they use.

Step 3. Find out who is responsible for hiring photographers or buying photographic services. You can do this by telephone or by mail, but the phone is usually the more efficient. If you have on your list a name from a directory, telephone and ask for that person; if he or she is no longer there or has another job, ask to speak to the replacement. If you don't know a name, ask whoever answers the phone to connect you with the person responsible for hiring photographers or buying photographic services.

Step 4. Remember that *somebody* will be getting those photo jobs, and if you make good use of your information, it will probably be you.

BREAKING IN ... Michael Weiss

Michael Weiss, who was once a schoolteacher, is a studio photographer specializing in food and still life for a variety of large corporate clients and advertising agencies in New York City.

I got interested in photography very late—at the age of 26—which was my first mistake.

My wife and I were moving up to Connecticut from the city, and I very blissfully thought that when we moved I'd quit teaching and get a job as a photographer up there. I put together a portfolio of about ten 4 × 5 transparencies [made with] an old Speed Graphic camera that I bought from a retired wedding photographer and a couple of lights from Spiratone [equipment manufacturers and distributors in New York]. I spent the entire summer doing these ten pictures, sending them out for processing through a discount department store.

I found out about a large photo studio, and went to them to get a job. You did everything there: color processing for negatives, for transparencies; you did black-and-white processing, color printing, black-and-white printing, black-and-white multiple printing. They put me right in the darkroom, printing black and white; but I learned everything I could from the other photographers. At the end of a trial period, I was given the chance to shoot. I eventually became *the* still-life photographer in the studio. After about a year, we moved to Westchester.

When I left, my choices were: coming into New York City and getting an assistant job for $85 a week, or starting my own studio. I started my own studio. I took our wedding money, which amounted to three thousand dollars, and used it to buy the equipment I needed to at least fake it for a while. I spent a month or two shopping around the city to get the best prices. I bought the best equipment, and the difference in prices was incredible. Somebody would be selling it used for $100, and somebody down the block would be selling it new for $90.

I had a portfolio by now. Half of it had come out of actual jobs and the other half came about from samples—things I wanted to shoot. It was a very mixed bag. Out of New York, they don't look for you to specialize. You could do food, you could do corporate, you could do industrial—it didn't matter. I couldn't commit myself to a studio; so I set up everything in various parts of the house. I never let clients come there. They all thought I had a real studio.

Once I got the studio set up in Westchester, I looked up advertising agencies, of which there were one or two. I figured there had to be more; so I called the Chamber of Commerce. They sent me to the Advertising Club of Westchester. Most of the ad agencies up there belonged to it; so I went to one of their meetings and spoke to the president of the club. He gave me a list of them, with the names of the art directors. I started calling up the agencies and art studios in the area.

I made a lot of appointments. Besides the ad agencies, I called a lot of companies just through the Yellow Pages. I always asked for the ad manager—not for public relations, because I didn't want that kind of photography. I'd go up and show my portfolio and try to get work from them. Everybody made promises, of course, and everybody was impressed; but I only heard from a small percentage of them.

In the beginning, it's a very cold business. They not only don't know you exist; they don't really care. And they don't know that they need you. In fact, as far as they're concerned they *don't* need you, and you've got to convince them they do. Most people are content with what they're getting. They don't know there's something better for the same price. I got a little depressed; but as long as I was getting appointments, I was going to keep on.

I landed my first account on the day I decided to quit. I had gotten a call from Savin Business Machines. One of the agencies I had gone to see got a small job from them and gave it to me. That's where it all began.

Things started to break very quickly after the Savin job. Another agency I had been seeing for a long time called me one day and said, "How would you like a new account?"

I said, "Who is it?"

"Nestlé."

I almost fell off my chair. Here it is twelve years later, and I'm still doing Nestlé. We have a terrific relationship. That agency also brought in Duracell batteries.

After I saw that Savin was real and that they seemed to be coming along with a certain amount of money every month, I decided to take the chance and get a studio. Before that I really felt I had a lemonade stand. I felt like a kid out on the sidewalk—"Photographs, five cents." I felt that no one was taking me seriously. Now, at least the client could come to the shoot.

I found that one client was leading to another, and another. Nestlé's was pleased with my work...they would recommend me. I began to develop a reputation.

At this point, we had picked up some clients in New York [City] and one of Nestlé's agencies promised more work if we were located in the city. So after about a year and a half or so we moved down here.

The first thing you do is examine who you know and who might know someone in the business. I had a partner at that time whose father was a printer. He did printing for some of the agencies and knew some art directors very well. That was our first contact. They were willing to see us and help us out by showing us what some of the top photographers were doing. This was important, because at this time neither one of us had ever seen a really top-notch portfolio.

We learned a lot. Learned what we had to put into the portfolio and what we had to throw out. We learned very quickly that in the city people didn't accept books that had a little of everything—they wanted a lot of one thing. We built the portfolio by just thinking of ideas to shoot.

You have to have some push in this business. You have to have some nerve. And it helps to be ignorant—ignorant enough not to think of the consequences. You've got to be smart enough to think of the idea first, then go ahead and do it....

You're in the business of communicating. That's really what you're doing for a living.

The more experienced you become, the more control you have; but there are some things you can't really control. When I look at a shot in the ground glass, I want the final picture to look the way I see it there. I have to anticipate what Eastman Kodak's interpretation of this is going to be, and then the lab's interpretation of what color they think a product should be. Once it's out of your hands, you're praying that this emulsion is a good emulsion from Kodak, praying that the lab is going to process it properly and it's not going to come back with all sorts of fantastic color tones in there that you never anticipated and that never existed before it went to the lab.

So when you get it back, the heart always beats a little bit faster while you're opening up that box of chromes. It's a great feeling when you see it's there. Don't touch it. Don't breathe on it. Call the messenger.

CHAPTER 7

GETTING THE JOB

Experience is not what happens to you; it is what you do with what happens to you.

—ALDOUS HUXLEY

What makes a person decide that you're the one to do the work?

Whether it's an editorial feature, an ad, or an AV show, the photograph is what people see and remember. Your client's reputation and image are, for that one job, defined through your viewfinder. *That's* why it's hard to break into the business: clients want to be sure before they send you out on a job that you will handle it with professionalism; that they can count on you to care as much about the job as they do, whether you are a staff member or freelance.

How do you inspire this confidence?

It's a lot of things working together, and you have to be aware and in control of the total package: both the way you present your work and the way you present yourself.

One communications manager who has hired photographers to do assignments for American Express, Pitney Bowes, and General Electric, is Neal Tooni. He puts it this way:

> I judge [photographers] on how good the "book" [portfolio] is and whether it's the kind of photography I need. I did a lot of industrial stuff, and if the photographer showed me interiors or people at machinery or people in office situations—and they were good—then I'd consider him.
>
> But I would never buy a photographer's services on the work alone. If I didn't like [the photographer], if I didn't like

the way they were dressed, if I didn't like the way they looked
...even if the guy was good and I liked him, if I didn't think
the client would react well to this photographer, I wouldn't
use him.

I had one photographer I used a lot who was *real* good.
His price was always right; the work was excellent; but I
could never take him to a client because he was always
stoned. I liked working with him, and he gave me great work;
but if we had to meet with the client on the job, I'd always
use somebody else.

Once you have experience and a reputation, it becomes
easier to get the work because the client can see that somebody
else has taken a risk on you and it's worked out well. They can see
that from your samples, from the list of clients you have, and from
the confidence you show at the interview. But the problem remains: how to get those first jobs. Let's take the process step by
step, from initial contact to dressing for the interview to what you
put in your portfolio.

FIRST CONTACT: TELEPHONE OR MAIL?

There are two schools of thought on this. Some people
believe that mailing a letter or sample to a potential client makes
it easier to telephone them for an appointment: They've already
seen your work, and if it interests them, you're halfway home. If
they misjudge your work from the image you send them, however,
or decide even before they see you that they can't use you, you're
out before you even get to first base.

Therefore, we recommend that as your marketing tool of
preference you turn to the telephone first, mailing a sample as a
follow-up to an interview or if they request it. (We'll look at how to
prepare a mailer a little further on.) The first step is to take the
list of names of buyers and companies you got from the reference
books and call for appointments.

Remember that if you have neither a name of a person nor a
specific department that buys photography, you can ask the receptionist for either the advertising department or public relations.
The receptionist will probably transfer you to a secretary in that
department, usually the secretary to the person in charge. When
you reach this secretary, remember she (or he) can help you and

usually will. Say that you're a photographer and would like to mail a sample to the person in the department who buys photo services. (Whether you have anything to mail or not isn't important. This is an unthreatening way to get the person's name.) Once you have the name, you can either ask if that person is available now to talk to you, or you can call them back later and just ask for them by name.

This is not as easy as it sounds. We know that. Don't take it personally if it's difficult to reach the person on the phone. If they have work to give you, *of course* they'll be busy and not able to talk to every photographer who calls. Maintaining friendly relationships with assistants can be very helpful in getting through eventually, though.

Jeff Cooper, an art director for the large New York advertising agency Benton and Bowles, told us:

> In the last year or so, I've seen a lot more photographers. There seems to be a lot of them popping up. I used to have the attitude, "I'll see anybody." But more and more frequently, I just don't have the time. I'm telling more and more photographers that I'm not looking at books. It's not that I don't want to. I enjoy looking at work, because it's fun seeing what some guy does for himself—get ideas—see new lighting—see where somebody is taking a chance. But you just can't when you get real busy.
>
> The stumbling block at big agencies for a new photographer is [the question] "why take the chance?" Because you don't have to. You've got a big budget; so go out and hire somebody who has a big studio that functions very efficiently—and quickly. Get the job shot, get back to the agency, get the photo out for a dye or retouching or whatever, and on to the next job.
>
> But when you get into a smaller agency or something like direct mail or catalogs, there's less concern, less pressure at the shooting. These are the places that new photographers should approach.

Preparing a mailer

Since you're working in a visual medium, the mailer is an important representation of your work. Take the time to do it right. The design, the photograph, and the text (if any) should all be tailored to the people you want to impress. Remember that photo buyers in large markets get hundreds of mailers.

One young freelance designer who has worked at some top New York design studios, Dan Taylor, explains the mailers from the receiver's point of view:

> There are just some things that are well put together. A photographer is usually not a designer; so he has someone else design it. As soon as you get it, you can see that a designer has figured out how to handle the material. If a mailer comes in and it looks like everybody else's, it just gets tossed. A lot of people use shots that are, by now, clichés. If you use a photo of an oil tanker, use it in a way that will make the designer say: "Hey, that's unusual. I've never seen that before." Any hint of amateurism in the design, the printing, even the envelope, and it'll never make it into their files.
>
> Spring is when they start reviewing photographers for the annual reports that will be coming up next fall. While they're in the final stages of an annual report, they really don't have time to see anyone. But at the end of March, April—I'd start sending them stuff again.

To get an idea of what professional photographers' mailers look like, scan a copy of *American Showcase* or *Corporate Photography Showcase*. Awards catalogs usually have a section on self-promotion that's good for clever ideas and inspiration. Appendix C of this guide lists these books and where you can find them.

Mailers are most effective as a series. This keeps your name in front of the buyer, demonstrates some of the work you've done lately, and, if nothing else, gives you another excuse to call and make your presence known.

It's a good idea to have a professional designer and printer handle the production of your mailer. If you have a friend who can do it, great. If not, ask the local printer to recommend someone. Maybe you can trade photography of design work for production of the mailer. You can try to work out a barter deal with the printer, too, but it might be difficult. They have a lot of people trying to trade their skills for free printing work and, in most cases, printers prefer cash.

THE INTERVIEW

This is the most important part of getting the job. You are selling your work, yes; but you are really selling yourself.

Any photography job means working with a team of people.

Nothing is created in a vacuum. In most cases, the person sitting across the desk from you at the interview will be the one working with you on the job. At this first meeting, he or she will be evaluating not only your work but also whether or not the two of you will work well together.

There's really no advice anybody can give you except "be honest." If you come across as fake, or pretend to be more experienced than you are, it shows. If (heaven forfend) you show somebody else's work as your own, they'll catch you on it.

Be honest, but with one big exception. If you feel unsure of yourself, intimidated, scared or nervous—which *everybody* does the first few times—fake it. (Some people we know recite all their strong points to themselves like a mantra before walking into a new office.) Project an image of confidence and professionalism. Deal positively and with enthusiasm with the people you meet. Don't ever fall into the trap of playing "ain't it awful" with a potential client or employer: They're allowed to complain about their jobs; you're not.

Above all, communicate your *enthusiasm* for photography in general and for this job in particular. This attitude, along with a good, competent portfolio, is the best approach to any interview.

Dressing for an interview

A brief comment on dress. There are no rules, because you are considered a creative person, in many cases dealing with other creative people. Style, in this situation, is a very individual matter. If you approach the subject with common sense and remember your mother's advice to always look neat and presentable, you will be right in most situations.

Résumé

In most cases, you will be getting work on the basis of your book or a mailer, as we discussed previously. If you're looking for a permanent staff job, or if the client asks to see it, you'll need a résumé. Prepare one early, so that you can just drop a copy in the mail when the need comes up.

In composing your résumé, it is important to direct it to a specific type of job or employment. Photo buyers are not usually interested in your restaurant experience or camp counselor work unless it had something to do with photography (coaching the campers on how to use their Instamatics, for example). They are, however, interested in the companies you have worked for, things you have had published, and awards you have won. Your education, related or not, should also be included. Any shows of your work during school, or work on a school paper or yearbook, will indicate that you've been working at photography for quite some time.

Update your résumé regularly. Include the best of your recent experience and eliminate the earlier, less impressive stuff. Your goal is a résumé that shows you to be competent and experienced.

Your résumé alone will not get you a job; it should interest the reader enough to call you in for an interview, though. Your entire life story, interesting as it no doubt is, is not necessary. Restrict your résumé to one page unless you are specifically asked for a "curriculum vitae." (This is a request for the entire story of your life, and is mercifully rare.)

THE PORTFOLIO, OR "BOOK"

The portfolio is the most important part of getting work as a photographer. We will refer to the portfolio as a "book," the term commonly used in the business of photography.

The best books are planned and aimed at a specific market. The buyer representing that market could be the head of photographic services at a local company, a magazine picture editor, or an art director at B.B.D.&O. You can reach all of them best by showing them something that relates to pictures they have used in the past. Remember the research you did in Chapter 6? The pictures you saw will be your guide here. Keep in mind that what you saw there was commissioned by someone, and that it was shot by a photographer no different from you. Somebody is going to do those jobs. It might as well be you.

Your book demonstrates your technical abilities, style, experience, and potential. On a more subtle level, it reveals your artistic taste, your approach to your work, and your work habits. In some cases you will be asked to drop it off and leave it for review. Sometimes you will have to send samples through the mail. In both instances, your book will have to speak for itself. It will *be* you to whoever sees it. Its form, content, and structure are very important. The time and money you spend now putting it together will be repaid many times over.

Here are the basic principles of assembling a book:

1. Technical excellence is assumed by any buyer. Do not give them reason to doubt your competence. Every shot should be sharp, properly exposed, well composed, and correctly color balanced. Prints should be "spotted" and any other needed retouching done; slides should be clean and mounts spotless. In short, neatness counts. Take no chances on this score. Make no excuses.
2. The physical format of the book is important. Appropriate forms differ from one specialty to another and are usually based on the final use of the picture. The section that follows this will give you general guidelines on books (or portfolios) for some major specialties.
3. Include only your best work. Be ruthless with yourself. It's better to show ten absolute knockout shots than ten great, five mediocre, and four not so hot. An uneven portfolio casts doubt on your ability to tell an interesting, useful photograph from a so-so one. Some people say you are judged by your worst picture; they are right.
4. The saying goes, "You get what you show." Show only the kind of work you want to do more of.
5. Show pictures the buyer can understand. Use your research here to make sure you have the kind of pictures they use. The more your presentation is directed toward one buyer, the better your chances of success. Don't show landscapes to a heavy-equipment manufacturer—show him workers in machine shops, or his product in use.

Formats for different markets

Advertising. The best choice here is a binder of 14 × 17 in. (36 × 43 cm) or larger with looseleaf transparent pages to hold samples of actual printed ads (known as *tear sheets*). When you are just starting out, of course, you won't have any tear sheets yet. But don't panic. The binder is still a good idea, and so is the size. You can fill it with either color or black-and-white prints up to 11 × 14 in. (28 cm × 36 cm) and the viewer won't have to turn the book to look at the horizontals. The important point here is that *the longest side of the largest print you show should be the same size as (or smaller than) the shortest side of the book.*

The large size has become quite common and is a result of the large prints needed by retouchers. Larger prints also add impact to the image.

You should also show original large-format transparencies (usually called *chromes*) in black cardboard mounts, even though the 35mm transparency ("slide") is much more common now, even in advertising, than it used to be. Most art directors prefer to see slides in plastic sheets or black cardboard group mounts rather than in trays. That way, they can look at several at a time on a light table rather than projecting them one by one. Bring a loupe (a small high-powered magnifier for looking at small things), so that he or she can see what they're looking at. (Make sure you have it when you leave, too. Art directors have notorious reputations as loupe borrowers.)

Your tear sheets are often irreplaceable, so you should make every effort to protect them. One way is to have them laminated, or bonded to a thin plastic film. It is usually best to have this done professionally with clear (not textured) and rigid plastic. Other methods are to have color photostats made, or to photograph the tear sheets and then have C-prints or Cibachromes made for use in the book. If a stat or a print is damaged, you can easily replace it. You will lose some quality this way; but the added security may be worth it. All you really need from the tear sheets is proof that your work has been published.

Audiovisual. No question here at all. 35mm slides, all *horizontal*, in a Kodak Carousel tray. These slides will often be projected on a huge screen, where every tiny imperfection shows. Make sure they are surgically clean and razor sharp.

Corporate/Industrial. Here again, 35mm seems to be the format of choice for most color work. Most corporate buyers and design houses are willing to project your samples, so the Carousel tray is the best choice for slides. Along with the tray, you should show any published work you may have (annual reports, brochures, etc.), either as tear sheets or in place in the publication. Some photographers also include original black-and-white prints in their presentation. If you have large-format transparencies that haven't been published, present them mounted in black cardboard.

Since so much corporate work is done in 35mm, some photographers copy their published work, black-and-white prints, and large-format chromes onto slides. They can then carry just one tray instead of a tray and a book. This makes things easier for both parties and is especially useful when you must leave your book with a buyer. If asked, you can always supply the originals (you can, can't you?).

Photojournalism/Editorial. Prints and tear sheets presented in a binder 11 × 14 in. to 16 × 20 in. (28 × 36 cm to 41 × 51 cm) and slides mounted in black cardboard are the preferred presentations here. Prints may be as small as 8 × 10 in. (20 × 25 cm). This is the easiest way for editors to handle your work and allows them to see it in a form close to the way they will be using it. If you have very little published work, this also allows you to create layouts of your photo stories to give them added impact. You can cut text away from published pictures, leaving only captions, then arrange these on a page. Clip the publication's logo (including title and date of publication) and position it at the top.

Sequencing the portfolio

Once you have decided which pictures you will use and in which format you will present them, you must put them in a sequence. The most common error in sequencing is the tendency to try to build to a big finish. There's nothing wrong with a big finish, but without a big beginning few people will ever see it. Without a doubt, the most important image in any book is the very first. The person looking at your book has seen hundreds, maybe thousands, of pictures in the previous week, possibly in the previous day. You must get his or her attention immediately. Start with your strongest image. This shot should knock their eyes out. It is the one that will identify you, your style and technical ability, to that viewer.

All work in a book should be grouped. A journalist might have all his personality portraits in one section, spot news in another, and feature stories in another. Whatever your specialty, keep related pictures together. It gives the viewer a good idea of your approach to a subject or a situation.

The presentation should flow naturally from beginning to end. There should be a sense of pacing and drama in its structure. Lead your audience through the book in such a way that they will want to see more. Be careful when you must mix vertical and horizontal images because it can be something of a visual shock to go rapidly from one to the other: In a slide show, try to keep at least three of each format together; in a binder, remember to use a size larger than your prints to avoid having to turn the book.

End with another of your strongest images. This one will also be sure to stay in the viewer's mind. It should end the book's sequence on a positive note. This image will be the starting point for your conversation with the person you have come to sell.

Building a book from scratch

In the beginning you will have no tear sheets or published work. You'll have to convince the photo buyers you can do professional-quality work of the type they use. "How do I do this?" you might well ask. One of the best ways is to do as Robert McCabe, a top New York still-life photographer, did. "I just went through *The Black Book*, photographic annuals, and awards books," he explains. "Found images that I liked and then tried a different approach to improve on them, as if I'd been given that same job to do."

Almost all the photographers we talked to built their book through self-assignments. If the image is strong, nobody is going to care whether you were on an assignment when you took it. In fact, even when on assignment, it's a good idea to shoot "one for them and one for me"—but only, of course, if there's time and you won't be shortchanging the client. Your first responsibility is to give them good work so they'll come back to you. The old maxim that a client in the hand is worth two in the bush applies here.

Monica Cipnic, picture editor of *Popular Photography* magazine and *Popular Photography Annual* summed up this way the question of what your portfolio should show:

> I want to see something I've never seen before. I want to know: What did you bring to this shot, other than the camera? I want to see how you interpreted the situation. So I'm looking for the most imaginative, the best work from every aspect, in a certain field.
>
> Before you go see anybody, you'd better do a little homework on their business: What have they shown, what kind of work do they want? If you're working with a very conservative company, don't show them something that they're going to object to—and then complain that they don't like your work.
>
> Don't give me something that *almost* makes it, because you feel sentimental about it. You've got to be tough. You've got to feel that someone who is cold and objective is looking at your work. Be ruthless.

THE "REP"

A "rep" is a representative, someone who sells another person's services or work and takes a commission on the sale. A good rep can make a big difference in certain markets, but a good rep is the hardest thing for a beginning photographer to find. In fact, most reps will not even talk to you until you are already well established and have a substantial client list and income.

You don't need a rep if: you work in other than a major market (New York, Los Angeles, Chicago, Atlanta, Dallas, Houston, etc.); you have regular clients and maintain a steady relationship with them; your potential market is *outside* the large advertising agencies.

You do need a rep if: you want to go after the top level of business in a major market; you want to increase your business substantially; you have difficulty selling your own work; you want to sell your work in another city. The ideal rep should have the charm of a movie star, the savvy of a politician, the discretion of a diplomat, and the financial cunning of a snake-oil salesman.

Good reps will ask for 25 percent of the fees they negotiate, and a percentage of "house accounts"—the jobs you got by yourself. Since repping is a profession, they are interested in representing photographers who have a good track record, photographers who are very saleable. A good rep functions as more than a salesperson (though to many photographers that is enough of an advantage). Many of them act as business managers and as marketing consultants, too.

There are those who say that if you get a good rep you are guaranteed success. The facts seem to agree. It's sometimes harder to make it without one, but many photographers do.

BREAKING IN . . . Garry Lancaster

Now a senior art director at the Ogilvy and Mather advertising agency office in Atlanta, Garry Lancaster has also worked for major advertising agencies in St. Louis and Nashville.

Most of our accounts are service industries and business-to-business. We have a hospital account, a restaurant, a bank, a regional division of an international travel agency, a producer of herbicides, a paper-products division of a conglomerate, and a mixture of similar accounts.

I usually do two shoots a week, using mostly local Atlanta photographers. There are some really good ones here. Quite a few of them went to the Art Center School in California. If we were shooting food, we might go to New York or Chicago; but for [specialists in] people or table-tops we stay right here. There is very little fashion work in Atlanta. Most of the photographers here are pretty versatile.

I have narrowed my photographers down to about three or four people that I use most of the time. Then you develop a really good rapport with the photographer and he knows what to expect from you. It's a good relationship, and you know you're not going to have any problems later on. I am so busy I don't have time to worry about whether the photographs are going to be great. They've got to be great every time.

I see new photographers, and I tend to try some of them on small jobs. One photographer I use now came in about two years ago. We tried him on a couple of things, and they came out just great. I just kept on using him and we've developed a good working relationship. That doesn't always happen. You have to be careful. You can get yourself into an awful lot of trouble using photographers you don't know.

That's the trouble with using an out-of-town photographer. But in some cases you've got to do it: If I'm going to some place not too far I'll take somebody from here; but in the major cities, or in situations where we can't afford the travel [expenses], I'll use a photographer there. I'll either use someone I've worked with before or someone who has been recommended to me. Sometimes I'll use *The Black Book* or the *Showcase*.

There are tons of photographers here—I must see a new book every week. But many of them are mediocre. I'm amazed at what they'll put in their books; they'll have three good pieces and then they'll put in a bad one. I can't tell if they just don't know it's bad, or what. A lot of photographers lately make the mistake of using too many gimmicks instead of just shooting a good photograph that tells a story. I like a picture that creates some emotion.

We use stock [existing photographs] for accounts where there isn't the money or the time to go out and shoot the picture. We use stock out of New York and some stock houses locally. Sometimes a photographer will be known for a particular type of work, and we will call him for stock [from his files]; it is very difficult to get good stock for some of our clients.

The best way to reach me is just to call, but reps tend to drive you nuts—I would rather speak to the photographer. A lot of photographers make the mistake of starting out in business and right away letting a rep sell them instead of doing it themselves.

Atlanta is fortunate to have as much talent here as it does. In fact, photographers have begun to move here from Los Angeles. Some photographers here have even been getting work out of New York.

CHAPTER 8

DOING THE JOB

"Work!?"

—MAYNARD G. KREBS

All the time, thought, and energy you've applied so far will be wasted unless you are able to complete and deliver a job successfully. That means, as the bottom line, that the client likes the pictures, sends you the check, and wants to use you again.

On the surface it would seem that all you really have to do is go out there, have a good time shooting what they tell you to, and have it processed. Well, yes and no.

Most clients do not know precisely what they want in a particular shot or group of shots. It's part of your job to help them decide, or decide (tactfully) for them if they can't make up their minds. All technical, aesthetic, and logistical problems are up to you. Control of and responsibility for everything that happens at a shooting—whether in the studio or on location—is yours. You will supply the energy and a lot of the taste and judgment required by any shot. You must create on demand and on deadline. Finally, you must make money on all this.

"But the cars, the houses, the girls or boys, the *fame* at least," you ask, "where do you mention all that?" Later, much later. Right now, let's talk about what makes the difference between success and failure on the job.

PREPARATION

The most important element in doing any job is planning. The better prepared you are for what you need to do, the more confident you will feel. If you feel confident, so will everybody else involved in the project. It helps things go smoothly and carries all of you over the surprises you come across during the shoot. On the other hand, if you really don't have any idea what you're doing, if you are unsure of some critical piece of equipment, point of technique, or even what the client really wants from the job, a subtle sense of panic settles in on everybody on the shoot. They may not know what it is or where it's coming from, but they will feel it, and this will affect the shoot.

A professional approach eliminates or minimizes the unexpected, and so helps free everyone not only to work but also to enjoy themselves in creating a worthwhile photograph. It is based on logic, asking the right questions, and, like the Boy Scouts, being prepared. Here are some guidelines to take you through the job from start to finish.

What do they really want?

When someone calls you and asks you to do a job—and here we mean any job in any specialty—you have to find out what they want you to do.

That's not as simple as it sounds. Many photographers have made the mistake of assuming the client meant one thing, while the client assumed the photographer understood something else altogether. The consequences can be pretty scary. Just imagine what it could be like once you are on location on an oil rig 50 miles offshore with the wrong film and inadequate lighting equipment. You could always fish or go swimming or something till the chopper comes back for you...

Don't be afraid to ask questions. Clients appreciate it because it shows you're as interested as they are. They like to see that kind of concern and involvement. In fact, it helps them think more clearly about what they want and usually results in a better job all around.

Here are some—not all, every job is different—things to consider when first talking to a client. Many of these points also have a bearing on what you will charge for a given job. (We will consider pricing in the next chapter; for now we're just trying to understand the assignment.)

Ask the client to describe the job. While you're talking about it, you'll probably start to get involved in the concept. Let your enthusiasm show. Excitement is good for you. The energy needed to create a good working situation can begin right here with this conversation. Make sure to cover any of the points listed below that apply to your job. Remember that these questions are not intended as a complete list but rather as a stimulus to get you thinking in the right direction.

JOB CHECKLIST

1. What format should this be shot in?
2. Is it to be in color or in black and white?
3. In which medium is it going to be used? (magazine, newspaper, slide show, exhibition prints, etc.)
4. What purpose will it serve? (advertising, picture story, public relations, gift to relative, etc.)
5. What should be included in the shot?
6. Is there anything that should be left out?
7. What, exactly, do you want to say in the picture?
8. How many people will be in the picture?
9. Do we need models? Who will cast them?
10. Where will the shoot take place?
11. How many locations are there? or special studio sets?
12. Whom can I contact at each location?
13. Are any special effects involved?
14. Do you anticipate any problems with the subject, location, etc.?
15. Is there any pertinent background information I should have?
16. When must it be shot?
17. When must it be delivered?
18. Who will represent the client at the shoot?
19. Who will bring the beer?
20. What is the budget for this job?

You get the idea. By the time you say goodbye you should understand the requirements and purpose of the job completely. Many photographers will submit a detailed, written estimate of costs for the job at this point. It is a good idea because during this conversation you will have also discussed money and reached an agreement on price (see Chapter 9).

MAKING IT WORK

The next step is yours alone. It is at this point that you function as professional problem solver/miracle worker. Based on the requirements of the job, you must now decide just how you want to do it and what equipment and materials you will need. Take into account the aesthetic as well as the technical problems. To do this, think the job through from beginning to end. Actually do the job in your mind: Anticipate the problems and solve them before they happen. It is almost impossible to be overprepared.

You also have to keep track of what you've done during the shoot. The best way to do this is to keep a detailed record on a "shot record." An example appears in Appendix H, page 174.

Studio

If you are working in the studio, these are some of the things you should consider:

1. How large an area must be shown in the photograph?
2. What background or surface should be used?
3. What props are necessary?
4. How will it be lit?
5. Will the shoot require extra personnel (stylist, home economist, special-effects rigger, makeup and/or hair person, extra assistants, etc.)?
6. What equipment (lenses, camera bodies, lights, etc.) will be needed?
7. Will it require special equipment? If so, do you have it? or can you rent it? Can you bill the rental?
8. Which film will you use?

Location

If you will be shooting on location, consider all the above plus a few more details. Remember, this is not a complete list. Each situation has its own requirements.

1. How far away is the location? Can it be scouted?
2. How long will you be there?
3. Must you take everything, or can you rent some equipment there?
4. Who knows where the place is and how to get there?
5. Who is making the travel arrangements?
6. Do you have enough cases to pack everything?
7. Are there any customs, visa, or other foreign travel problems?
8. What kind of light exists at the location? What lighting equipment will you need?

9. What kind of electrical power is available? Will you need a generator?
10. Is there a contact person at the location? Get home phone numbers for people involved. Not everything occurs during business hours.
11. Will you need any special clothing (cold-weather, wet- or heat-protective; hard hat; bullet-proof vest; tuxedo, etc.)?
12. On outdoor locations, who approves schedule or cost changes due to bad weather?

Getting it going

These lists could go on forever. We aren't attempting to create the ultimate job checklist, just to give you an idea of what you're going to be expected to handle routinely. Professional photography requires careful attention to detail, technical savvy, artistic ability, and nerves of titanium.

Once all this is sorted out and the people involved finally get together for the shoot, the job begins to take on a life of its own. The momentum you and the client get going in that initial contact will accelerate during the shooting. When things are going just right you can almost hear a hum of work and concentration in the air. This totally focused activity—the way you feel while you're doing it and the pictures that result—is the real payoff for the professional. Whether it is a single journalist on a long assignment in some remote part of the world, a fashion photographer shooting with a crew of ten, a school photographer working his way through the senior class, or somebody making the chairman of the board look better than he ever has in his life—the good photographers all feel something similar.

However good it feels, though, you can't lose sight of what you're there to do: create pleasing or informative images for other people. Your art is needed to bring life to their ideas. It is a very satisfying thing to do well. After all, if we only did this for the money we could have been stockbrokers, right?

Model releases

If there are any people in the pictures you shot for commercial use, all of them should sign model releases. A model release is simply a document in which a person whose likeness can be recognized in a picture legally assigns someone else the right to use that image in some way. The release may state a specific and limited use or, more commonly, it will be a general release permitting any use including advertising. Without a release you can (and probably will) be sued for invasion of privacy. The release must be signed by the person in the picture unless he or she is a minor, in which case a parent or guardian must sign.

It is always good practice to get a release from anyone in a photo whenever you can, even if you are just out shooting for yourself. You may want to sell that shot of two people jogging in the park through a stock agency. Most people will be flattered and happy to sign a release.

We have included a simple, but legal, release in the Appendix. It was supplied to us by Phillip Leonian, who intended it to be less intimidating than many other forms now in use.

AFTER THE SHOOT

Once everything is shot and you have chromes or contact sheets, you are at last close to being finished. Editing is a very important part of any job. Your selection from the total "take" will represent your best efforts. First eliminate all technically unusable shots from a take before the buyer gets a chance to see any of them. (Your client may have been in the business much longer than you have and knows that of course you will bracket, and of course a couple of shots might be out of focus. Even so, no buyer likes to see anything but the best: Any reminder of possible mistakes seems to scare them a little.)

Get the results to the buyer on or (we can all dream, can't we?) before the deadline. Make sure that everything is in the right form: proper size of prints, slides in boxes or in sleeves—whatever you agreed to beforehand. These little touches are a further proof of your consistency and professionalism. Make that guy feel good. Show respect for your work and his ideas by treating the final product well.

Once the work has reached the client and they've had a chance to look at it, give them a phone call. Try not to glow with pride too much, but ask how they liked it. Be confident, but concerned. You are making sure they think of you when they think of your kind of work.

Now we come to the other payoff. Move on to the next chapter to unlock the mysteries of billing and getting paid.

BREAKING IN . . . Garry Gold

Garry Gold is a commercial photographer working in Albany, New York. He works with both advertising and corporate clients. He is also the photo editor of Indy Car Racing.

The whole psychology of a market this size is to be a jack-of-all-trades. If I were only a food photographer, for example, I would do two jobs a year here. That's what's appealing about it. The fact that no two or three days in a row are ever the same, and the real boring stuff that comes in here I know will also go out of here in not more than a day.

The name of the game is that you're doing a lot of different kinds of work, and you have to have the equipment to handle it. You've either got to own it yourself or have access to it through other photographers, because there's just no rental market. What happens is that you associate with other photographers. There are guys in this area that borrow some of my gear and I borrow from them. They're your competition, but it's a matter of knowing you're going to get caught sometime; so you have to keep the door open. Once you've got the job and you're out there doing it, nobody's going to just let you hang if you need something.

If you looked at the Yellow Pages around here you'd think there were fifty advertising agencies, but there are actually about twenty that use photographers. Seventy percent of my income is derived from the agencies within 25 miles of my door. The other 30 percent is direct to companies and those clients are probably within five miles of my house.

I haven't yet done any direct mail [promotion for myself]. I don't do any advertising. I'm not even in the Yellow Pages. People who call a photographer out of the Yellow Pages tend to ask, first, how much it costs and, second, "How come it's so much?" It's all word-of-mouth, and half of that is because art directors move around so much. I'll do some things for someone at one shop, and the next thing you know they're someplace else. You can still work for the first place, but now you're working for the second one, too. There are also some freelance designers who pass me around. Most of the work has been developed this way.

The average day-rate for a commercial photographer in this area is between $400 and $500. We have our one New York biller who's closer to $800. He's from the city and has a New York portfolio and trades on that psychology. He's able to get $800 from the larger corporate clients who are used to paying that, no matter where they are. The rest of us try to bump up our rates for those clients; but by and large you average around $500. Billables include film, processing and materials—sometimes the assistant, sometimes not. All the rest of the stuff out of the A.S.M.P. book. You can't bill for cancellation quite as easily if they give you any notice at all. There is no such animal as overtime, but you might bump your day rate up.

I bill a day rate, and that usually gets someone anywhere from eight to ten hours. As we approach that ten-hour mark, I start adding on so much per hour, or a day and a half—that kind of thing. I stay pretty flexible. There are certainly other games in town; so you have to stay flexible. Sometimes you can price better than someone else because of the equipment you own. If you can do certain things or do them quicker because of it, or make a shot that's that much different because of the equipment, you're in a better position to get that job.

Right at the beginning I found that good work delivered on time beats great work delivered late. Great work is something that they're prepared to deal with, but late work is impossible.

Assistants are in pretty short supply because the schools in this area don't have any photo programs that teach technique. There're a lot of people that talk about assisting. Usually they can load your car, but they can't load a 4 × 5 film holder. So you find somebody who wants to go ahead and work and isn't planning on being a photographer two weeks after he's done a job for you, telling people he's a shooter. You keep him. You find a way to make him happy.

One thing that I've made a point of is knowing all the processes involved—not just the part that I do. And I find that in a lot of cases that's why I get hired back. Because my overall concern for the job, not just my end of it, helps them deliver a better product. You become a resource for a small client, who comes in and says, "We'd like to do the following." So you start getting an idea of what they want and say, "Well, have you talked to a printer? Have you talked to a designer? How are you going to run it?" Then, when you start doing the work for them, you know that they'll come back to you because you helped out—you didn't give them something that they had to spend more money on to change before they could use it.

Part of my mixed bag is that I was always interested in car racing and, even at school, shooting sports and that whole student activity scene. So as a way to get into these things, I'd drag the camera, with less interest in taking the picture but more in just wanting to go.

What turned the corner for me is that I realized I just couldn't keep on doing this as a hobby at these car races. I started to pursue the appropriate markets, the major magazines and the drivers and stuff. A lot of it is being at the right place at the right time. An organization called CART (Championship Auto Racing Teams) has broken off from USAC (United States Automobile Club) and set up their own organization and series of races. I got involved with a couple of people who were reporting on that. . . . We pitched them to do an annual, an end-of-the-season wrap-up. They liked the idea and helped underwrite it to a certain extent, and that was our entree. We are now doing a magazine, editorially totally independent from them, and continuing to do their official annual publication. I'm the photo editor and it's really a lot of fun. We are becoming the source of information for that kind of racing at a time when it's really growing.

CHAPTER 9

GETTING PAID FOR
THE JOB

There is a very important business decision that you will face before you even get to do the job: "What do I charge for my work?"

Pricing creative work is almost as much of an art as doing it. You need to take several factors into consideration and strike a balance among them. The ideal is a balance that makes both the photographer and the client happy. Your experience and knowledge are the first part of the equation.

Experience counts

Experience comes into it in two ways. First, the more experienced you are the better your reputation and the more impressive your "book." These things allow you to charge higher fees. Second, as you gain experience in working with buyers of your services, you begin to understand the pressures they are under, their working style, budget restrictions, and other factors influencing them. This understanding makes it easier to set a price on your services that gives you a profit and doesn't scare off your client.

Experience will also tell you when a buyer is trying to get a job done for too low a price. This is often a problem with people who hire photographers who are just starting out. When you run into this situation, take into account what you might get out of the job that will compensate for the lack of money. Resist the immediate impulse to say, "Forget it, jerk. Shoot it yourself!" or words to that effect. It may yield particularly good samples for your portfolio. It may get you noticed by an editor you have been trying to reach. It may involve extensive expense-paid travel. Take all these things into consideration. Don't, however, take too many jobs like this or you will be out of business before you really get started. A situation to avoid is the notorious, "I'll make it up to you on the next one." We're all still waiting.

A real danger in taking jobs for excessively low rates, even if you are able to make a profit at it, is that you will be thought of as The Cheap Photographer. This is a distinction you do not want. It is difficult to impossible to raise your rates for a given client if they know you will work for less.

The solution to this dilemma lies in the fact that there are many buyers of photography. When you start out, you will get the small jobs with the low budgets. That's natural. You are an unknown quantity and don't have the samples to prove your competence. As your experience increases and your book grows, you will go to new buyers and present yourself, truthfully, as a more experienced professional asking higher rates.

You can then go back to your original clients (the ones who only used you because you were cheap) with your new book. Most of them will be delighted you have done so well. Some will even brag they gave you your first jobs. (Use a little restraint here unless you have the bail money on you.)

THE GOING RATE: WHICH MARKET?

Most freelance photographers in advertising, corporate, architecture, and, in a modified form, photojournalism charge what is termed a *day rate;* that is, a certain amount of money for a day's work.

The day rate is only a fee and does not include expenses, such as film, processing, travel, models, helicopter rental, treatment of gunshot wounds, etc. All these expenses are billed to the client. The fee is determined by how the photographs are being used. Remember that the photographer is selling only *use* of the picture. He or she owns all rights to the photograph except those assigned to the client for payment of a specified fee. (This is covered in more detail later in the chapter, under the heading Use.)

An exception to the day rate is the per-shot rate often paid for catalog work or for some product shots in smaller markets. This rate usually includes all expenses.

In freelance photojournalism, a day rate is usually regarded as an advance against space use: A magazine will pay a certain amount of money for one-time rights to reproduce a page of photographs, and this is called a *page rate*. It is usually equivalent to the day rate. It's a good deal, because if they like the shoot they may use more than one page. You are then paid for everything used, minus the advance. You will never be paid less than the advance; so you can't lose. (Of course, this does not apply to staff photographers, who are on the publication's regular payroll.)

Portrait and wedding studios use a different rate structure, one that reflects the retail nature of their business. Typical studios charge a sitting fee (which may include a certain number of prints) followed by a per-print charge. Their studio expenses are factored into these prices. They also use package deals, "loss leaders," extra-cost options, and all the other marketing tricks of the retail trade. (These pictures remain the copyright property of the photographer, but they cannot be used for advertising or display without a model release.) Studios may also sell frames, copy and restoration services, and albums and provide photo-finishing services.

Your prices will be primarily determined by the "going rate." This is the price usually paid, in your area of the country, for the kind of photographic work the client wants and for the way it will be used.

THE GOING RATE: WHAT'S YOUR LEVEL?

Some typical rates are listed in the table in Appendix A. These are only guidelines. Rates vary widely within each field. They vary for each part of the country. They vary by experience level. They vary by client. There is no way to tell you specifically what to charge.

You can, however, find out for yourself.

Ask other photographers doing similar work what their rates are; in general, you will find them to be helpful. Most remember what it was like to start out—how confusing it can be. Ask them about clients you will be approaching: What are they used to getting for certain kinds of work? What rights does that price usually include? This is not entirely altruistic on their part. They realize that if you know the going rate, you will be less likely to undercut their generally accepted prices. This is good for them, and it is also good for you: Keeping prices at a reasonable level makes it possible for all of us to make a living.

Look at the ranges of rates in Appendix A and, when you get a little more experience and confidence, try quoting the higher one. If no one turns white and gasps, you may have just raised your rate.

Of all the buyers of photography we talked to—big companies and small, large ad agencies and two-man shops—not one said they were scared off by a price that was higher than they were used to paying. If they liked the work, they would negotiate and try to hire the photographer for what they had in the budget.

At first glance, some of the day rates people charge may seem high to you, especially if you have another job or other income that takes care of your living expenses. In fact, they are quite reasonable when you analyze them in light of the cost of doing business.

COSTING FACTORS

Overhead

In order to find out whether the rates you charge will let you make a healthy profit, just break even, or put you out of business, you need to know what it costs you to do business.

These unbillable expenses are known as *overhead*.

To figure your overhead, simply identify your costs. (You can use the list that follows.) Enter a yearly amount for each category. If we have left out something that applies to your business, add that, too. Remember, these are business expenses *only*. If you work out of your five-room house and use one room solely for business, only 20 percent of your rent should be entered here. This also means you can list only 20 percent of your utilities or any other expenses associated with your home. Telephone expenses in this case are probably mostly business: Take a look at a typical month's bill and figure it out.

You get the idea. You're not sending this to the I.R.S.; so there's no need for it to be correct to the penny. Add all of this up, and what you have is your overhead—fixed overhead plus operations not billable to a specific client. You must make at least this amount of money to stay in business.

OVERHEAD/OPERATING COSTS
(other than photographic equipment)

Space (rental of studio, office)	_____
Utilities	_____
Telephone	_____
Car	_____
Insurance	_____
Repairs	_____
Office supplies	_____
Salaries (assistant, secretary, etc.)	_____
Fees (lawyer, accountant, etc.)	_____
Promotion (portfolio, advertising, mailers, etc.)	_____
Studio supplies (background, tape, gels, etc.)	_____
Entertainment (business only)	_____
Travel (unbillable but business-related)	_____
Depreciation (equipment, real estate)	_____
Taxes (sales, use, etc.)	_____
Miscellaneous	_____
	TOTAL: _____ .

Note: Your gross income, of course, would include direct shoot-related expenses, which are eventually billed to the client but for which you must often lay out the money up front. It is difficult to figure these into your operating expenses because they can be as little as one roll of film or as much as a month on location. You might add a figure under Miscellaneous that could represent what you might spend here.

Profit margin

These are your business costs. But in order to survive, you must also make a profit. How much profit you make is a function of your fees, multiplied by the number of jobs you do, less this overhead. Just for your own information, make a rough estimate of how much income, above your overhead, you need to go after to maintain your present standard of living. Add this to your overhead. You have just created your first business goal.

Now go a little further and project how many jobs you might do in a year. Divide this number into your overhead-plus-income figure. The answer will tell you how much you should charge for each job (averaged overall) in order to cover your overhead and produce an acceptable profit.

Try it with a couple of different projections. The answers should make it fairly obvious why you don't want to be known as "that cheap photographer" for very long.

WHAT YOU SELL: USES AND RIGHTS

How the photographs are used is an important factor in determining the fee. In general, a standard day rate assumes one-time use in a specified medium (like an annual report or an ad).

The more widely distributed the medium, the higher the price. Company newsletters with a small circulation pay less than promotional brochures that will be distributed to most of a company's current and prospective customers. Advertising, which reaches an even larger audience, pays still more.

For example, a photographer might be hired by a company to portray a new facility for a brochure. Let's say it is a small company and a middle-level photographer. The day rate might be between $400 and $600. The invoice would read something like this: *For one-time brochure use only*. If the photographs were to be used in a national trade ad, the photographer might charge between $700 and $1000 for the shooting day and put on his invoice: *For one-time national trade advertisement use only*.

It is necessary to determine ahead of time what the intended use is. You can sell any or all rights to your work. It is a good idea to keep as many of them as possible, however.

If the pictures were originally for a brochure and later the client decided they were perfect for a trade ad, you would be entitled to extra payment for that extra use. How much you are paid depends on use alone, since the pictures already exist. This is why it is important to specify the agreed-upon use *on the invoice*.

Yes, that means exactly what you think it does. When you do a job for a client, the client does not automatically own all the pictures, for any use, forever, amen. In fact, according to the current copyright law, *you*, not the client, own the images, in spite of the fact that the client paid you to make them and paid for the supplies and expenses of doing so. The law protects you and your creative work. (Staff photographers are an exception. As full-time employees, their work belongs to their employer. This is known as work for hire.) That's a very basic description of complex legislation. We recommend that you read "Copyright and Practice of the Trade," by Phillip and Edith Leonian, reprinted in Appendix F.

You will run across clients who insist on owning all rights. Sometimes a work-for-hire clause which assigns copyright to the client will be printed on the back of a purchase order. Large corporations are notorious for this. Outside of major markets, buyers are sometimes uninformed and seem surprised that there is any question about it. You don't, of course, have to take the job. But, when you are trying to break into the field, *No* is a hard word to say. Weigh the pros—money, more work, samples, experience—against the drawbacks. Only if it is worth it to you, really worth it, grit your teeth and take it. If it isn't, turn it down and go on to the next one.

Under those circumstances you may want to do some shooting for yourself, too. Make sure you keep some good stock and good samples for yourself. Not that the client shouldn't get the pick of the first-rate material, you understand; just shoot enough so there's something for everybody.

In a retail portrait or wedding business, rights and use are generally more straightforward. The buyer usually wants the pictures only for personal use and is buying prints—the physical objects. The studio retains the negatives (that is, the created image) and all reprints are ordered from you. Prices will be based on this assumption. Occasionally a portrait studio may do executive portraits for local businesses. In this case, all the use considerations of other commercial work apply.

NEGOTIATING A PRICE

Keep all these things in mind when it comes to the moment of truth and the person across the desk says, "What would you charge for something like this?"

In some cases there is little or no negotiation involved. With a portrait studio, for example, the prices are set. In photojournalism the page rate is often predetermined, and negotiation would only be necessary if you had a one-of-a-kind picture (the attempted assassination of a head of state, for example) or have won a Pulitzer Prize and become a "name." Even advertising budgets are usually decided long before an art director calls in a photographer.

Sometimes you can just ask, "What's in the budget?" If they tell you and it sounds reasonable, that's your price. If they won't tell you, ask for something in the neighborhood of the going rate.

Have a price in mind that is your bottom line, and be prepared to turn down work that does not pay. You can't negotiate if you don't know when to say, "I'm sorry, but I can't do the job for that price." (That's a nice way to say, "No, you cheapskate.")

Consider some other factors when setting your price for a particular job. At first your major objective is just to work. This will often mean barely breaking even. Because of this, you should try to get as much nonmonetary compensation out of the job as you can. Shoot for your "book." Shoot the job several different ways. If a small job has given you access to a location otherwise closed to you, use the opportunity to shot for yourself once the job is done. You may even be able to sell these pictures to the client later, or use them to get more work from him at a better rate. In short: hustle, and make the most of every situation.

Always do your best work. Even when you are working cheap. You cannot afford to have anything shabby out there with your name on it. The clients should feel they're getting more than their money's worth. You are building trust and good will that will work for you through referrals and repeat business. Then you can charge what you're really worth.

Talk, listen, write

Perhaps the most important point in pricing is the phrase, "Agree up front." Never surprise a client with a bill much larger than he thought it was going to be. When you set a price on a job, you should work with the client to estimate what it will cost to do it; that is, your fee plus all projected expenses.

Suppose you give someone a price of $250 a day for, say, two days to shoot a small brochure on a new manufacturing process. You agree that expenses, film, and processing, will be extra. But if you don't discuss the nature of those expenses and a probable price range, then rent a car and some lenses, hire two assistants, and have the shoot catered, you are going to be in trouble.

By the same token, you will be less than pleased if one of the shots from that same job shows up not only in the brochure but also in a national ad. This has happened.

Both of these situations are ugly and both could have been avoided. The best policy is to agree about every facet of the job in advance and *in writing*. This not only minimizes the possibility of later problems but also helps you plan the shoot. Use the list of billable expenses on the A.S.M.P. and A.P.A./SPAR forms in Appendix B as a guide.

The indefinite job

Use can become a problem with some buyers. Beware the person who says, "We're not sure; just shoot it." That usually means they want all rights and will use it forever. Be careful here to keep negotiations on a positive note. Phillip Leonian puts it this way:

> If they want all those rights they can pay for them; you're willing to negotiate for them. But there's a way to make it cheaper [by buying just the rights they need]. It's not blackmail. Tell them, "Some photographers don't care what you do with their work, but I value mine."

Edith Leonian continues:

> Particularly when you're dealing with new clients, one of the things that makes it seem more difficult is the business of making sure that they know what they're buying or what the price covers and not doing that in a negative way.... You don't just say, "It'll cost you [such-and-such]." You say, "A picture for use in [whatever it is] for one year costs [such-and-such]." That's professionalism.

Markup

It is common practice to mark up the cost of goods and services you purchase to do a job. That is, if film costs you $5.00 a roll, it is not unreasonable to bill it at $5.50: a 10 percent markup. This is designed to compensate, to some extent, for your time in buying the materials and expending your cash for materials that will be reimbursed. Travel and living expenses are not customarily marked up.

Most clients understand and agree with this practice. Others do not, and will go so far as to avoid hiring a photographer who marks up the materials. To figure out what goes on in your area, ask other photographers. *Don't* discuss it with the client. Markup is usually not part of negotiation.

Negotiation checklist

Some major points to be discussed and agreed on in advance are the following:

- Detailed description of job (color? studio? aerials? number of days? etc.)

- Any special arrangements on your part
- Any special arrangements on client's part
- Location, where shoot is to be done
- Amount of film to be shot, including processing and Polaroid (estimated)
- Rental equipment to be paid for by client
- Rental equipment to be paid for by you
- Who pays for assistant(s), other support personnel
- Deadline (preliminary conference, final choice, delivery date)
- Purpose (promotion, technical, advertising, etc.)
- Who, from client, will be on shoot?
- Who has final approval of the pictures?
- Your fee
- Advance (a reasonable request if it's a large job, will take a long time, or requires a large outlay for materials and expenses)
- When will payment be made (on delivery?, 10 days?, 30 days?)

GET IT IN WRITING

Once you've agreed, get it in writing. You may want to use a printed estimate form similar to the one developed by the Advertising Photographers of America (A.P.A.) and the Society of Artist and Photographer Representatives (SPAR) or that of the American Society of Magazine Photographers (A.S.M.P.). Both are reproduced in Appendix B. You could also simply type an estimate on your letterhead. Nobody should object to this: it protects both parties from subsequent misunderstandings.

Make it clear that this is an estimate only and not a firm quotation. An estimate is an approximation of projected costs and may change with unforeseen conditions, whereas a price quotation is binding for the job. But be as accurate as you can. A reputation for going over budget is as damaging as a reputation for losing film.

Get a purchase order or letter of confirmation from the client. The purchase order (P.O.) should include description, estimate of total cost, and deadline information, at least. This, along with your estimate, eliminates any guesswork about what is required when and how much it is going to cost.

If you see from your estimate that you will have to lay out a considerable amount of money to do the job, ask for an advance. This is a reasonable request. In most cases you will have to wait at least 30 days (in some cases much longer) to be reimbursed.

All these are important points to settle to make sure you'll get paid what the job is worth. Until it's proven otherwise, assume that your client is a reasonable person who is used to dealing in a professional manner. Learn to "read" your clients so as to present your terms in a manner they can accept. Sometimes you will have to accept a little less, sometimes you will get a little more. In a business conducted among people, everything is negotiable: Make the best deal you can for yourself, taking the variables into account. Just remember that you are trying to work with people and not against them. Coming on like a terrorist who is holding Cleveland hostage will get you nowhere.

BILLING

Now, let's assume that you have agreed on a price, then shot and delivered the job. How do you get your money?

You send a bill, also known as an *invoice*, to the client. The client gets the invoice and then (eventually) sends you a check for the full amount.

Most of the time it really does work this way. In order to make sure the process works like this for you, here are a few procedures you should follow:

STEP BY STEP

Step 1. Type the invoice either on your letterhead or on a printed invoice form such as the A.P.A./SPAR or A.S.M.P. form reproduced in this book. If you use a form, you can adapt it to suit your business. Either way, your business name and address should be printed at the top.

Step 2. The invoice should be dated the day it is prepared.

Step 3. Invoices should be numbered in a consecutive series. This will let you know quickly how many jobs you have done in a given period, and it's an easy way to identify a particular invoice. It is a good idea not to start your numbering sequence with a naked "1" because it's a little scary for a client to get invoice No. 5 from someone he's just entrusted a very important job to. Aside from that, number them any way you want.

Step 4. Include the client's job number and/or purchase order number.

Step 5. Note the date(s) on which the shoot took place.

Step 6. State clearly what use the pictures are intended for and what reproduction rights are granted to the client.

Step 7. In the body of the invoice, list your fee first.

Step 8. Next, itemize all expenses. If an item comprises more than one unit (10 rolls of film, for example), cite the unit cost as well as the total amount. You will probably be required to include receipts for your travel and living expenses. (The client will want the originals; so be sure to keep a copy of such receipts for your records.) A list of billable expenses appears on the forms.

Step 9. When you have filled in the applicable ones, add together all the fees and expenses. If there are no taxes or other additions or deductions, this is the total balance due. If there are other considerations, this is a subtotal.

Step 10. If there are any applicable taxes, compute them and add the total in this line. Total this amount.

Step 11. If you have received an advance or any other payment on the job, deduct it from this total.

Step 12. Finally, show the TOTAL BALANCE DUE. This is what the client owes you.

Invoice forms

Examples of a simple letterhead invoice can be found in the Appendix. It's not very elaborate, but it gets the job done. The two other longer forms are the ones mentioned before, the most comprehensive such forms now in use. They were developed by New York advertising and editorial professionals, both photographers and reps, and so are best suited to similar markets and specialties. Not every job will fill in every blank in the comprehensive listings of billable expenses; so don't let its length scare you off. Take a good look at it. Even if it is too much for you now or doesn't apply exactly to your situation, you can't beat it as a checklist. Some beginning photographers find that using a form adds to their professional image.

The back of the forms list terms and conditions that apply to various aspects of the assignment. Read them carefully, keeping in mind the market for which these forms were designed. In reality, as a new photographer, some of these provisions (like copyright) will always apply. But others (like overtime) may have to wait awhile. These conditions can be printed or stamped on the back of your letterhead invoices. Their presence on the invoice will give you at least some protection from the unethical client. Start out assuming that all of them apply, but remember that everything is negotiable. If you give something up, you should get something in return.

When to bill

Prepare and send out the invoice as soon as the job as been delivered and approved. You should receive payment in about 30 days. (Some companies send out checks only once a month. Find out what your client's billing cycle is and submit your invoice at an appropriate time. If you miss the cycle you may have to wait another month.)

If you don't receive a check in a month, you can send a statement to the client listing outstanding amounts, or you can call your contact person there and politely mention that you have not yet received payment. *Be calm.* You can't afford to lose clients at first, even slow-paying ones. After 60 days you have a right to get a little excited. By this time you should reasonably start to wonder if they plan to pay you at all. Again, other photographers are your best source of information about the client. Find out the name of the person who is directly responsible for paying the company's bills. Usually a call to this person will straighten everything out. If it doesn't, call your lawyer and proceed from there.

BREAKING IN...
Frank White/Susan Mansfield

Frank White does corporate, editorial and advertising photography. Susan Mansfield is his rep, business manager, and wife. They are based in southern Connecticut.

Susan: You have to *be* a business. I think you have to accept that. You have to be a business and you have to run it like a business or you aren't going to last very long. You can have all the talent in the world, but if you don't have any kind of a business mind yourself, get a support system—somebody working with you or for you with some business sense.

Frank: I started out working as an assistant with ex-*Life* photographers. *Life* had folded in 1972, and these guys were just starting out in business on their own. So in addition to assisting and learning some technique, I was also watching these guys fumble in business. It wasn't till later on that I figured out that I learned quite a bit from that experience.

One of the people I was assisting took a job as photo editor of a new magazine, which turned out to be *People.* I had assisted him for two years. He knew what my abilities were. Well, *People* magazine turned into a great success. I immediately went in to try to get work from him. I'd go in there and talk to him and he'd say, "Look, I'd like to give you a break but there's absolutely no way I can. There's just too many people here that have paid their dues that I've got to use."

But I'd go to his office and wait and talk to him between phone calls. I would shoot stories in the style of *People* magazine to show him, and he would look and say, "Good stuff. Fine. But I'm not going to use you."

Assignments would come in . . . and his job would be to figure out who would best be able to shoot this assignment. I was in there talking to him one day and an assignment came in. A little nothing shot; just a head shot. But he got on the phone and he called every photographer he had on his list in New York City. They were all out of town. He started calling people in the Midwest. He was going to fly them in to come and shoot a head shot, and here I am sitting in his office. I didn't say anything. Without exaggeration he must have been on the phone for half an hour. Finally, . . . he looks over and he says, "Okay, do it."

The shot was a photograph of a young woman. Instead of shooting it on 35mm, I checked out all the strobes the magazine had and shot it on large format. I just did a number on that shot. This girl was totally overwhelmed. I came back, they processed the film, it looked good, and they gave me another assignment. Then more after that.

The magazine was new and I was in kind of on the ground floor. I was identified with it, and that established me in a certain slot. It was a very lucky break that made it easier to break into the corporate market.

Susan: The work that you do for a magazine probably gives you more visibility and credibility than any other. It's probably a bigger break to get a spread in *Money* magazine than it is to get a spread in an annual report—even if you're going after corporate work.

To find the buyers, you just look in the books. You make lists. You call them. You make notes. You figure out ways to get through to them. There are certain things, though, that you discover after a while. Like: Some guys come in at 8:30, their secretary gets there at 9; and the secretary will never let you through. So you call at 8:30. Sometimes you call at 6 at night. There is no list that's going to tell you that. You'll have to figure it out yourself for your specific needs.

Whenever Frank had something really good, like the *Sports Illustrated* cover, I sent the whole magazine to agencies in Connecticut and it worked really well—we got all kinds of work.

Frank: If you're going to get into the business you have to be prepared for the long haul. There are a handful of people that are just going to break on the scene and establish themselves right away. But for every one like that, there are hundreds of very successful photographers who only got to that point through years of hacking away.

Susan: It's true in magazines, it's true in advertising, it's true in corporate work: You've got to get the experience. You've got to knock on the smaller doors. You're much more likely to get work and be able to build the portfolio.

I used to think there would come a time when we could

say, "Well, okay, we've made it. They know us. I don't have to go out anymore." And to an extent it's true. There are many times when I call now and they say, "Oh, yeah, we know who Frank White is" or "We've seen his work." But you can never relax. You always have to be out there. Even with your current clients you have to keep re-instilling that you're good, you're current, you're active.

CHAPTER 10

IF YOU FREELANCE

Our dictionary defines a freelancer as *one who pursues a profession without long-term contractual commitments to any one employer.* If only it were that simple.

In the real world it means that you are an independent contractor providing a service—in this case, photography. As such, you must function the way any small business does. That is, you need to create an image, make sales, bill for your work, keep financial records, pay business taxes, provide for your own pension and insurance, promote yourself or advertise, deliver high quality work, and *make a profit.* You will notice that nowhere have we mentioned trips to Tahiti or Rolls-Royces. In all fairness, though, it must be said that most of the photographers making those trips and driving those cars are freelancers. (When we say "freelancers" we are including studio owners but excluding people who work for salary.) They are the top of the profession, of course; but if you are looking for that kind of success, this is the only way to go.

There is virtually no limit to what you can learn as a freelance photographer. The limits that do exist are usually imposed by geographical location and specialty. *Location,* because the larger markets tend to have more work and higher budgets. Smaller markets, on the other hand, tend to have lower costs of living and of doing business, which may counterbalance the lower fees. *Specialty,* because some kinds of work simply pay better than others. Unfortunately these fields usually have the highest overhead and the most competition. (See chart back in Chapter 1.)

In any case, if you have decided on a specialty or specialties and want to go out on your own, there are some decisions you must make and some steps you must take before you see your first hard-earned dollar. The rest of this chapter will outline the start-up of an independent photography business. The information is designed to cover small-market studios as well as the big-market freelancer, since the basics of business vary little across the field.

FINANCIAL FOUNDATIONS

Money is the root of all business. Before you decide to go into competition with your boss, make sure you won't have to ask for your job back in six months. Without an adequate financial base, a photography business is just as doomed to failure as a restaurant or a gas station. You must assume that, like other small businesses, you will make little if any money in the first year (maybe two) you are in business. This means that you must be able to buy all the necessary equipment and to locate yourself. You also need money for operating expenses to support yourself, your family, and pets—as well as pay your business expenses—for this period of time. That's a lot of peanut-butter sandwiches.

Capital

There are many ways to do this. One of the most common is to start a photography business while holding another job that pays the basic expenses. This is not easy. Conflicts will arise constantly. But it has been done, and the discipline it requires will serve you well. (In fact, Alfred Stieglitz once said, "If you want to be a photographer, get a job wrapping packages at Macy's.")

It is possible to do it halfway, working on weekends and evenings as a part-time photographer. If this is the way you decide to go, you will still need to follow the procedures for setting yourself up as a business. In fact, a part-time business can be a significant tax advantage.

If you decide that professional photography is really what you want to do, though, you will have to give up that other job: You cannot be a top success unless you are fully committed to your business. There is a sense of purpose (some say terror) in being out on your own that you never quite feel if you know your rent is paid. This can be crucial motivation to building a business.

Some people are able to save enough to get themselves started. Others are bankrolled through loans from family or other backers. Sometimes a spouse with a steady job will keep the landlord at bay. However you go about getting it, this money is an investment in your business. It can pay dividends only if you spend it wisely. Plan how you will use it and try not to get carried away with nonessentials.

Credit

Credit is a necessity in business. You will need credit at your lab and with some of your other suppliers. Credit cards are indispensable for travel and entertainment. (Ever try to rent a car without one?) The sooner you start to build a credit history the better off you are. Perhaps the easiest way to do this—besides paying your utility bills on time—is to open a charge account at either a local department store or one of your friendly suppliers. Use these accounts judiciously and always pay on time. They do keep records of when you pay, and consistent lateness can come back to haunt you.

If you have a job when you start out, apply immediately for credit cards. You have a pretty good chance of getting a Visa or a MasterCard through your bank, but only if you are employed. Once you are totally on your own, they probably will not give you one, but they will not take it away if you already have it.

Treat your credit with care. In the beginning there is always a temptation to abuse it a bit. If you're not careful, a few dinners and a new lens or two will lead to the letter requesting that you cut the card in half and send it back. This letter will seriously inhibit your ability to do business, so avoid it.

SETTING UP IN BUSINESS: LOCATION

Now that you know what you want to do and have the money to do it, you'll have to decide where you will have the best chance of success. This will depend greatly on your specialization(s) and ambition. If you want to open a portrait-and-wedding studio and your town already has three, check out nearby communities to see if there might be a need there. If you are going into fashion and want to do only that, you'll want to head for the large metropolitan markets.

Ambition plays a part here: Not everyone wants to do battle in the offices of New York or Los Angeles. If you do, you'd better want to reach the top because the dues you pay will be very high. If you don't care for high tension, you might be able to rise to the top in another area with less competition, equal satisfaction, and maybe proportionately higher rewards.

Smaller markets, as we've pointed out previously, require less specialization. You can shoot, say, still life, fashion, and portraits whenever the need arises without having to choose one and do only that. No less dedication is required to making a go of it in Wichita than in Chicago, of course, but fewer people will be competing for the same business. Only your own skills and personality can help you decide.

If you can't get the work or satisfaction you want where you are now, then go immediately to the best large market for your kind of work and get a job as an assistant. The experience you gain, even if you don't stay, will be worth it. There are more and more successful photographers outside the big cities who have gotten their training there and moved. This trend will continue as the sheer number of working professionals increases.

Keep in mind that the photographer who goes to the big city from the small town should allow plenty of time and money to build a business. He must become familiar with the quirks of doing business there, consistently create work that will be saleable there, and build a network of contacts. This tends to take less time in the smaller marketplaces, and therefore requires less financial investment.

In some specialties—notably journalism, travel, and corporate photography—it is not unusual for a photographer to operate from a relatively remote location yet have an agent or a group of steady clients in not one but several big-market areas. Very often these photographers have spent some time in a city making contacts and developing a reputation. Once established, they can get work consistently without the high costs of a city-based business.

SETTING UP IN BUSINESS: ORGANIZATION

In order to function legally as a business and to provide an image of professionalism and reliability to clients, there are certain things you must do.

First of all you must decide on the legal form your business is to take. There are three basic choices: sole proprietorship, partnership, or incorporation.

Sole proprietorship. This means that you not only own the business, you *are* the business. Everything that the business owns is yours, and vice versa. Unfortunately, this includes debts and lawsuits. You are personally liable for any proceedings brought against the business. All income from the business is taxed as your income, but you may deduct business expenses from your taxes. This is the simplest business form and the one most used by beginning and part-time photographers.

Partnership. A partnership is a multiple proprietorship. Legal and tax procedures are about the same as for sole proprietorships, except that two or more people are the business. Partnerships are very attractive to beginning professionals because they allow photographers to pool their money, equipment, and contacts to mutual advantage. At least in the ideal, it's to their mutual advantage. Both partners are liable for the debts of the partnership, no matter who incurred them.

Sometimes as business develops, so do personality clashes. One partner may feel the other has taken advantage—and battles start. Successful long-time partnerships do exist, but they are rare. A setup where two photographers share a facility, and maybe some equipment, but function as separate businesses seems to work out better.

There are various forms of partnership; one of them may be right for your situation. For example, you may know someone who is willing to bankroll you, but you want to keep control of the day-to-day operation of the business. A limited partnership arrangement exists for just this sort of thing. Any partnership deal should be handled through a knowledgeable attorney to avoid expensive errors.

Incorporation. This step is almost a necessity if your yearly net income (after all expenses, including your salary) exceeds $35,000. If you expect to get sued or to leave a lot of debts, it limits your liability to the assets of the corporation. In general, incorporation holds no advantages to the newly started photography business.

Starting on your own

We suggest a sole proprietorship when you first start out. It is the simplest to deal with, and if things don't work out it's the easiest to dissolve. You can always change your form of business later if your income warrants it.

Before you make any decisions about your form of doing business, check with a friendly local attorney or accountant. If possible, talk to someone who knows the status of photographic business in your area.

FIRST STEPS

There are some bureaucratic details you must attend to, to make yourself A Business in the eyes of God and the I.R.S. If you have decided on sole proprietorship, you should complete the following steps:

Get a D.B.A. This is a document usually acquired from your county clerk's office. With it, you register the fact that you, John Smith, are *Doing Business As* "John Smith Photography" or "Great Shots Studios" or any other name not obscene or already in use by someone else.

While you are at the county courthouse, find out if there are any local or state regulations governing photographers. In most states you can do business without interference, but some require various licenses or permits. Get these now if you need them.

Open a business account. Call on some commercial banks in town and tell them you are a new business and you want to open a business checking account. Find out from each all the terms, conditions, special deals, rates, and all other information pertaining to this type of account. Pick the one that sounds like the best deal. Armed with the D.B.A. documents, go to that bank and open an account. Thereafter, use this checkbook for all business-related expenses and never for anything strictly personal. This might seem a little difficult at first, but at the end of the year the checkbook will be a clear record of your business dealings—very important around the middle of April.

File for a tax number. In most states and some cities the business of photography is subject to sales tax. The rules and regulations for this are complicated, and they differ in every locale. Get in touch with your state and city sales tax bureaus and comply with their requirements. In most cases, after filling out some forms you will be issued an identifying number. You can then buy certain equipment and supplies without paying the sales tax. Unfortunately, you will later become an agent of the state, because you will have to collect sales tax from your clients and 'pay it to the state. Failure to do this can be very expensive and may cause you to have to deal with a class of people not famous for their understanding or sense of humor—tax collectors.

An accountant who specializes in work for photographers and models has a few words of caution about sales tax. Listen to Joe Taranto:

> You have to be careful with sales tax. There's no uniform sales tax law. In different states, different activities are taxable. The best thing to do is to go to the local state sales tax office, explain what you do, and they will give you guidance.
>
> Don't listen to what the photographer next door does. If he gets caught, that gives you nothing. At least if you go to the state sales tax office and get the name of the person you talk to, you've made the effort. Maybe you'll make an honest mistake, but at least you made a sincere inquiry.
>
> Unlike income tax, where you can sit there and say well, maybe 50 percent is deductible rather than 25 percent and it becomes a give-and-take with your auditor, sales tax is an absolute. It's a certain percentage, and that's that. If you didn't collect, you're still liable.

LOOKING THE PART

Now that you are legitimate in the eyes of the law, you have to appear so to your prospective customers. This involves creating an image of professionalism and reliability in the way you present yourself and carry out your business dealings. To do this, you will need a few simple things.

Business cards

These are perhaps the most basic form of advertising and promotion in existence. People will see your cards more often than any other promotional piece you use. You will leave them after interviews, pass them out at parties, and give them to people to give to other people. They will be referred to for your phone number and your address. Properly used, they will get you work.

Cards can work for you only if they are well designed and printed. A card that looks amateurish or is poorly produced will do you more harm than good. The design and production of your card are indications of your taste and influence the way you are thought of as a photographer.

Look at the cards used by photographers and other business people in your area. Ask around to find out which printers give the best quality for a good price. The ideal is to have your card designed for you by an experienced designer. When you're starting out, this might be beyond your means unless you have a designer friend. If you have to do it yourself, get some help from the printer who is going to produce the cards. Often they will have samples of standard business cards they can print quickly and more cheaply than a custom-designed one. At the beginning this could be a good choice. Pick a color in the grays, tans, or whites (avoid day-glo) and a relatively heavy stock. Remember to keep it simple: Elaborate type and cute little pictures of guys with cameras confuse the issue.

Letterhead and envelopes

Along with your cards, your letterhead and envelope project your business image. A poor design on cheap paper will work against you every time. Remember that your bills, estimates, bids, and any correspondence to your clients will be typed on this stuff. They, for the most part, are in businesses that deal in quality design, printing, and paper. They know what good is and they like to be impressed. You probably won't lose any jobs just because of tacky stationery, but you can never tell, can you?

While you're at the printer's about your cards, ask about letterhead designs and paper stocks. Once again, he may have standard designs that could fit your needs and in fact match the typeface, design, and color of your cards. It's a good idea to pick them all out at the same time.

Rubber stamps

Rubber stamps? Absolutely. You should have at least one and probably two rubber stamps. One is for slides, to fit the following information on the wider border of a 2 × 2 cardboard mount:

© 19 ____ Your Name
Your Phone Number
Your Address

The other stamp, for prints, will have the same information in larger type.

The copyright line—© 19 ____ Your Name—is a must to protect your ownership of your work and its reproduction rights. The date can be left blank and filled in by hand, but the easiest way is to start with the current year and get a new stamp at the beginning of the next. Do not allow any work to leave your hands without this notice or it is in danger of falling into public domain. The other two lines simply make it easy for someone to call you for additional prints or more work. (More on copyright later, but for now trust us and go get the stamps. The date can come after your name, if you prefer.)

Telephone-answering device

Nothing annoys a potential client more than to call a photorapher and get no answer. Most don't try again, they just go to the next number on their Rolodex. You must have some means of answering the phone when you are out. You have three basic choices here:

- Have someone in your office at all times to answer the phone. Unless you have a spouse or a live-in friend who's at home most of the time, this is probably out. It does have the advantage of a personal touch and clients appreciate this; but at the beginning, employing someone to answer your phones and act as secretary is an expense you can avoid.
- Contract with an answering service. This means that a live human being will answer your phone and take a message. You can call the service from any phone, at any time, to collect your messages. You can also leave messages for a specific person; and some services will provide wake-up calls. (Extra services usually mean extra charges.) It is cheaper than having a person in your office, and some services provide excellent performance. Use one that picks up when your phone rings instead of using a referral number: You are trying to be easy to reach, and another number means another step. A bad answering service—one that is slow, rude, or loses your messages—can work against you. Make sure the one you choose is doing its job.
- Get an answering machine. By now most of us are used to talking to machines. They are impersonal, but they seldom lose messages. You can use them, too, to screen calls when you just don't want to talk to certain people (creditors, for example). You only have to pay for them once. With a simple, direct message, they are hard to beat for getting the job done cheaply and efficiently, and with the remote controls now available you can check your messages from any telephone anywhere.

SETTING UP IN BUSINESS: PAPERWORK

A recent study shows that poor record keeping was a major contributing cause in 88 percent of all business failures. There is no need for you to be included in this number the next time these people publish their results.

Business records

The basic idea of record keeping is a simple one. You are keeping track of your money. You have to know how much there is, where it came from, and where it went. You will also need to account for it to the I.R.S. The only way to take all the deductions you're entitled to is by keeping proper records.

No complicated procedure is necessary for this. You can do it efficiently and simply with a few basic tools.

Your business checkbook. Try to pay all your business expenses by check. Keep a clear, detailed record on the stub of the amount, date, and reason for each check. If the expenditure was for a particular job or client, put the job number or client name on *both* the check and the stub. Keep all canceled checks.

Datebook/Expense diary. These are available in stationery stores in an almost infinite range of sizes and designs. The two basic types are a relatively large one for your desk and a smaller version that is carried with you. Both are useful, but we prefer the pocket size. It allows you to make notes of small cash outlays—cab fare, tolls, tips, emergency supplies—as they occur. It will also satisfy the I.R.S. requirement that you have both a receipt and a diary entry for all expenses greater than $25.

Accordion file. Use this to file your receipts. *Keep every receipt, no matter how small.* You may file them alphabetically or by any other means convenient to you, but you must have them to keep track of your expenses and to justify them at tax time. Credit-card receipts are especially valuable. If you have filled in the reason for the charge as well as other pertinent data, they are acceptable without further documentation.

Notebook or ledger. These records may be elaborate or simple—for the new sole proprietor, very simple. You should at least enter all income in one column and all expenses in another. At the end of the week—or month—total up each column to see how you stand. Nothing could be simpler. Later on, you may want to modify your books or have a system set up for you by an accountant; but this money-in/money-out system, though primitive, works pretty well when you're starting.

Job jackets. This is an excellent method of keeping track of what it has cost you to do a particular job. (No, it does not mean that you stuff all the receipts in your jacket pockets!) For each job, you have a manila envelope identified with the name and number of the job. Stuff all receipts, notes, layouts, purchase orders, and so on in there. Many photographers tape to the outside of the envelope a form on which they also enter expenses. This makes it easy to track your expenses as you go. An example of a job jacket appears in Appendix G.

Taxes

As a business, you are subject to various state and local taxes as well as to Federal taxes different from those applying to individuals. There is no way we could cover your tax situation fully in less than a separate book—not to mention the fact that the rules change a little every year. Our advice is to find an accountant, or at least a tax-preparation specialist who is familiar with the photography business. This person can help you set up your books and other accounting procedures and suggest ways to run your business so as to minimize you tax burden. These services could include helping you set up a tax-deferred retirement account (such as a Keogh or an Individual Retirement Account). In general, such experts pay for themselves.

Just to get you started, though, here are brief descriptions of three Federal forms you may not have seen before. You will have to use all of them when filing a tax return for a business.

Form 1040SE. If the taxes you owe for the year are more than $100 over any tax money that's been withheld for you, you must pay estimated taxes in advance four times a year on Form 1040SE.

Schedule C. This is where good business records will pay off on your taxes. The self-explanatory subtitle of this form is: *Profit or (Loss) From Business or Profession (Sole Proprietorship).* On it you will show all your business expenses and business income. Schedule C tells the I.R.S. the story of your business year.

Form 1099. Every company you work for as an independent contractor will send you a 1099. It tells the government how much you were paid by that company during the year. It's just one method of making sure you report all your income. The combined amount from all your 1099s and all your other business income will go on Schedule C.

Schedule SE. Since taxes are not withheld from business income, you will have to pay a Self-Employment Tax. It's the equivalent of the Social Security Tax taken out of a wage-earner's check; you just figure it out on this form.

And the good news

There are advantages as well as disadvantages to all this paperwork. As a business, you are entitled to deduct from your taxes the cost of goods and services that the Internal Revenue Service feels are legitimate operating expenses. You are allowed to depreciate business property and in some cases can actually deduct an investment tax credit from your taxes owed (not from your income). Exactly what can be deducted or what percentage of each item can be deducted is a gray area that keeps many attorneys, accountants, and Federal employees busy all year. A partial list of deductions follows (remember, this applies to *business* use only).

DEDUCTIBLE BUSINESS EXPENSES

Rent
Utilities
Telephone
Film
Processing
Paper
Chemistry
Travel
Publications (related
  to your business)
Education expenses
  (to advance in your
  business)
Advertising/Promotion

Accountant
Legal Fees
Insurance
Car/Car rental
Depreciation of
  equipment
Repairs and
  maintenance
Postage
Salaries
Entertainment
Business Gifts...

And that's only a partial list. All this applies whether you are a full-time or a part-time photographer, as long as you are a bona fide business making a profit in two years out of five. (You can even argue with them about this, but you will probably lose.)

Remember that, no matter who handles your taxes, you should understand what is being done. Even though the preparer must sign the tax form along with you, it is you, not the preparer, who must pay the penalties.

Here is a simplified tax preparation method. It sometimes seems like the one that the I.R.S. would prefer.

Insurance

"It was here a minute ago. I know it was. Did anybody see a silver case around here? The one that had *Expensive Photo Equipment, Handle With Care* painted on the side? *Who* picked it up? He was running?..." If you're lucky, the alarm clock will remove you from this nightmare. If not, your only hope is insurance.

Nobody likes to think about insurance. It's like betting against yourself. Unfortunately, it is necessary if you are to avoid personal and/or financial disaster. As a businessperson and a photographer, there are several kinds of insurance that may apply to you.

Camera floater. This is the one that would have saved you in the example. It's the policy that most photographers think of first. At best, these policies are written to cover loss or damage to equipment anywhere in the world and for almost any reason short of normal wear and nuclear attack. (Who would you collect from?) There are two basic types of coverage here. The most common is called *Actual Cash Value*. It will reimburse you for the purchase price of the item, less depreciation. The other version is *Full Replacement Cost* or *Stated Value* coverage, which will pay the amount listed on the policy regardless of depreciation.

Package policy. Your camera floater would most likely be attached to some form of package policy which would cover your business premises. This usually includes fire and theft and other coverages, such as *Loss of Use* and *Valuable Papers*. There are many options to this type of coverage. If you live where you work your household insurance may cover some of this, but it usually will not cover any item used in a business.

General liability. Here, you are covered for claims of injury to others resulting from your negligence. Coverage includes bodily injury at or away from the studio and can be extended to include legal injury, such as invasion of privacy, slander, and libel. In some states, anyone who works for you under your direction can be considered an employee, even if it is a freelance assistant who works for you only one day. Even if both of you consider the assistant to be an independent contractor, the law may see things differently. If you have regular employees, of course, you are required to have this coverage.

Bailee coverage. If you often photograph the property of others and it remains under your control for a period of time, you should consider this one. It will cover you if the $3000 watch you photographed for Tiffany's is stolen.

Medical insurance. As individuals applying for hospitalization and major medical insurance, we are generally discriminated against by the insurance industry. Group rates, even groups of four or five, are lower. Our only hope is to join an organization like the American Society of Magazine Photographers or Professional Photographers of America and take advantage of their group rates, which are better but still not great.

Shop around when you buy insurance. The difference in rates from agent to agent, for identical coverage, is amazing. Buy only what you think you need and can afford. Go for the high deductible to get the lowest rate. Most insurance agents are ethical, but some will try to sell you much more than you need. Remember that they work on commission.

APPENDICES

APPENDIX A

THE GOING RATES

The following tables show representative ranges of day or assignment rates and other fee structures. They are meant to be used only as a guide, since many factors must be taken into account in setting a price.

TYPE OF PHOTOGRAPHY	LOCAL	REGIONAL	NATIONAL
ADVERTISING			
Consumer Magazine	$350–600	$ 500–1500	$1000–3000
Trade and Newspaper	300–600	500–1000	750–2000
Billboards	500–1000	1000–1500	1500–2500
Package	300–600	750–1500	1000–2500
Point-of-Purchase	200–600	600–1200	1000–2500
Catalog or Brochure (per day)	300–600	600–1500	750–2000
Catalog or Brochure (per shot)	50–100	125–250	200–400
Album Cover	300–600	500–1000	750–2500
CORPORATE			
Annual Report	$300–600	$ 500–1000	$ 750–1500
Audiovisual and House Organ	250–500	350–600	500–1000
PUBLIC RELATIONS			
Press Kit, Party, Award (per day)	$200–350	$ 250–600	$ 350–750
Head shot, Etc. (per hour)	35–75	50–100	75–200
EDITORIAL			
Reportage	$150–250	$ 200–300	$ 250–700
Illustration	250–300	300–500	400–1000
Book and Magazine Covers	250–350	350–600	650–1500

PORTRAIT
Portrait photography is usually priced as a sitting fee plus a per-print charge. It is common practice to offer several types of sitting at different price levels.

TYPE OF SERVICE	RANGES OF AVERAGE FEES	
SITTING		
Economy	$15–50	
Standard	25–70	
Special	50–150	
COLOR PRINTS	**1 print**	**2 or more (each)**
5 × 7 in.	$20–50	$15–40
8 × 10 in.	30–85	15–50
11 × 14 in.	50–150	25–115

PRICING GUIDES

THE BLUE BOOK OF PHOTOGRAPHY PRICES
Photography Research Institute, Carson Endowment
21237 South Moneta Avenue, Carson, CA 90745

ESTIMATING MANUAL FOR PROFESSIONAL PHOTOGRAPHY
Professional Photographers West Executive Office
2245 North Lake Avenue, Altadena, CA 91101

APPENDIX B

BUSINESS FORMS

The forms in this section are described in Chapter 9, on doing business. They include:

1. Letterhead invoice sample
2. A.S.M.P. invoice form
3. A.P.A./SPAR estimate/invoice form
4. Simple model release
5. Longer model release
6. Property release.

Tod Bryant Location Photography

May 22, 1984

Big Oil Inc.

1234 Park Avenue

New York, NY 10022

Attention: Accounts Payable

INVOICE

TB84-123   BI Job #ARP-45678

Photography for Big Oil Inc. Annual Report 4/23/84 to 4/27/84

5 days photography @$1000/day....................$5000.00

78 rolls PKR 36
with processing @$10.50/ea....................... 819.00

10 rolls Polaroid type 52 @ 5.25/ea.............   52.50

                              sub total   5871.50

                              sales tax   484.40

                              sub total   6355.80

5 days assistant @$75/day....................... 375.00

5 days lunch (receipts attached)................. 108.25

car rental (receipts attached)................... 179.16

                         TOTAL $7018.21

PAYABLE UPON RECEIPT

212·929·8036 115 West 23rd. Street New York, New York 10011

Assignment Confirmation/
Estimate/Invoice Form

FROM: **TO:**

Date:
Subject:
Purchase Order No:
Client:
A.D./Editor
Shooting Date(s)
Our Job No:
☐ Assignment Confirmation
☐ Job Estimate
☐ Invoice

Expenses

ASSISTANTS	_____
CASTING	
Fee/Labor	_____
Film	_____
Transportation	_____
FILM & PROCESSING	
Black & White	_____
Color	_____
Polaroid	_____
Prints	_____
GROUND TRANSPORTATION	
Cabs	_____
Car Rentals &/or Mileage	_____
Other	_____
INSURANCE	
Liability	_____
Other	_____
LOCATION SEARCH	
Fee	_____
Labor	_____
Film	_____
Transportation	_____
LOCATION/STUDIO RENTAL	
MESENGERS & TRUCKING	
Local	_____
Long Distance	_____
SETS/PROPS/WARDROBE	
Set Design Fee	_____
Food	_____
Materials	_____
Props	_____
Set Construction	_____
Set Strike	_____
Surfaces	_____
Wardrobe	_____
Other	_____
SPECIAL EQUIPMENT	
SPECIALIST ASSISTANCE	
Electrician	_____
Hairdresser	_____
Home Economist	_____
Make-up Artist	_____
Stylist	_____
Other	_____
TALENT	
Adults	_____
Children	_____
Extras	_____
Animals	_____
TRAVEL	
Air Fares	_____
Meals	_____
Hotels	_____
Overweight Baggage	_____
MISCELLANEOUS	
Gratuities	_____
Shoot Meals	_____
Toll Telephone	_____
Other	_____
EXPENSE TOTAL	_____

Photography Fee(s) & Totals

$ _____

PRINCIPLE PHOTOGRAPHY (BASIC FEE)
($_____ per day or photograph, if applicable)

DESCRIPTION

SPACE &/OR USE RATE (IF HIGHER)
($ per page: $ per cover: $ per photo)
TRAVEL &/OR PREP DAYS (at $ per day)
PRODUCT OR SUBSIDIARY PHOTOGRAPHY _____
($ per photograph)
POSTPONEMENT/CANCELLATION/RESHOOT
(% of orig. fee)
WEATHER DAYS (at $ per day) _____

TOTAL FEE(S) _____
TOTAL EXPENSES (see 1st column) _____
FEE PLUS EXPENSES _____

SALES TAX (if applicable) _____

TOTAL _____

ADVANCE _____

BALANCE DUE _____

MEDIA USAGE

ADVERTISING		EDITORIAL/JOURNALISM	
Animatic	☐	Book Jacket	☐
Billboard	☐	Consumer Magazine	☐
Brochure	☐	Encyclopedia	☐
Catalog	☐	Film Strip	☐
Consumer Magazine	☐	Newspaper	☐
Newspaper	☐	Sunday Supplement	☐
Packaging	☐	Television	☐
Point of purchase	☐	Text Book	☐
Television	☐	Trade Book	☐
Trade Magazine	☐	Trade Magazine	☐
Other	☐	Other	☐

CORPORATE/INDUSTRIAL		PROMOTION & MISC.	
Album Cover	☐	Booklet	☐
Annual Report	☐	Brochure	☐
Brochure	☐	Calendar	☐
Film Strip	☐	Card	☐
House Organ	☐	Poster	☐
Trade Slide Show	☐	Press Kit	☐
Other	☐	Other	☐

Subject to all Terms on Reverse Side—Which Apply in All Cases Unless Objected to in Writing by the Sooner of the First Shooting Day or Ten Calendar Days. Usage Limited to Reproduction Rights Specified

Client Signature: _____

Terms and Conditions

(a) "Photographer" hereafter refers to (   ). Except where outright purchase is specified, all photographs and rights not expressly granted on reverse side remain the exclusive property of Photographer. All editorial use limited to one time in the edition and volume contemplated for this assignment. In all cases additional usage by client requires additional compensation and permission for use to be negotiated with Photographer.

(b) Absent outright purchase, client assumes insurer's liability to (1) indemnify Photographer for loss, damage, or misuse of any photograph(s) and (2) return all photographs prepaid and fully insured, safe and undamaged by bonded messenger, air freight or registered mail, within 30 days of publication. In any event, client agrees to return all unpublished material to Photographer in the above manner, and supply Photographer with two free copies of uses appearing in print.

(c) Reimbursement for loss or damage shall be determined by a photograph's reasonable value which shall be no less than $1500 per transparency or $_____ per print.

(d) Adjacent credit line for Photographer must accompany use, or invoice fee shall be tripled. Absent outright purchase, client will provide copyright protection on any use in the following form: "© photographer's name, year."

(e) Photographer has supplied or will supply specifically requested releases on photographs requiring same for use. Client will indemnify Photographer against all claims and expenses due to uses for which no release was requested in writing. Photographer's liability for all claims shall not, in any event, exceed the fee paid under this invoice.

(f) Time is of the essence for receipt of payment and return of photographs. Grant of right of usage is conditioned on payment. Payment required within 30 days of invoice; 2% per month service charge on unpaid balance is applied thereafter. Adjustment of amount, or terms, must be requested within 10 days of invoice receipt. All expense estimates subject to normal trade variance of 10%.

(g) Client may not assign or transfer this agreement. Only the specified terms, hereby incorporating Article 2 of the Uniform Commercial Code, and the 1976 Copyright Law are binding. No waiver is binding unless set forth in writing. Nonetheless, invoice may reflect, and client is bound by, oral authorizations for fees or expenses which could not be confirmed in writing due to immediate proximity of shooting.

(h) Any dispute regarding this agreement, including its validity, interpretation, performance, or breach, shall be arbitrated in (Photographer's City and State) under rules of the American Arbitration Association and the laws of (State of Arbitration). Judgment on the Arbitration award may be entered in the highest Federal or State Court having jurisdiction. Any dispute involving $1500 or less may be submitted, without arbitration, to any Court having jurisdiction thereof. Client shall pay all arbitration and court costs, reasonable Attorneys' fees plus legal interest on any award or judgement.

(i) Additional Specifications: (to be filled in as applicable)
Placement (cover, inside, etc. _____).
Size (½ page, 1 page double page, etc. _____).
Time limit on use _____ Use outside U.S. (if any) _____.
Copyright Credit Line is required in the following form: © 19____ (insert photographer's name).

(j) Client agrees that the above terms are made pursuant to Article 2 of the Uniform Commercial Code and agrees to be bound by same, including specifically clause (h) above to arbitrate disputes.

(k) Weather postponements and cancellations 48 hours prior to shooting, will be billed at ½ fee. Thereafter, full fee will be charged. All expenses, costs and charges shall be paid in full by the agency.

(l) Days put on hold at client or agency request and not cancelled within 24 hours will be billed at full fee. All expenses, costs and charges shall be paid in full by the agency.

(m) All cancellations after confirmation and/or booking a shooting date will be billed at ½ fee if cancellation is prior to 48 hours before shooting date, and full fee if cancelled less than 48 hours before shooting date. All expenses, costs and charges shall be paid in full by the agency.

(n) If same photograph that is cancelled is rescheduled for a later date, full fee will be charged for the actual shooting.

(o) The cost of all charges or deviations from the original layout or job description must be approved by the art director, art buyer or agency representative.

(p) The agency is responsible for sending an authorized representative to the shooting. If no representative is present, the agency must accept the photographers judgement as to the execution of the photograph.

(q) When shootings are booked on a day basis, the day rate shall apply to any consecutive 8 hour period. Any further time will be paid for on a pro-rated basis. All additional expenses (rentals, talent assistants, etc.) due to extended time shall be paid in full by the agency.

☐ ESTIMATE	☐ INVOICE	ESTIMATE VALID UNTIL _____

DATE:	STUDIO JOB/INVOICE#:
AGENCY P.O.#:	SHOOT DATE:
AGENCY JOB#:	ART DIRECTOR:
CLIENT PRODUCT:	ART BUYER:

MEDIA USAGE (REPRODUCTION/LICENSING RIGHTS)

		National	Regional	Local
Consumer Mag.	#			
Consumer Newsp.	#			
Trade Mag.	#			
Trade Newsp.	#			

PERIOD OF USE: _____
Subject to terms & conditions on reverse side.

☐ Double Page ☐ Annual Report
☐ Single Page ☐ Billboard
☐ ½ Page ☐ Book Cover
☐ Poster ☐ Brochure
☐ Test ☐ Catalog
☐ Television ☐ Packaging
☐ Album Cover ☐ Point of Purchase
☐ Photomatic ☐ Transit
☐ Editorial ☐ Other _____

DESCRIPTION:

COLOR:	B&W:	OTHER:	FORMAT:	STUDIO:	LOCATION:	SET:

CREATIVE FEES MAIN ILLUS.:   SECONDARY ILLUS.:

PREP: TRAVEL: SHOOT: WEATHER:

A CREW: STUDIO COORDINATOR: OVERTIME:

STYLIST: OVERTIME:

ASSISTANTS: OVERTIME:

MAKE-UP: HAIRDRESSER: OVERTIME:

HOME ECONOMIST: FOOD: FEES: TRANS:

B CASTING: FEES: FILM: TRANS: USE OF FILES:

C LOCATION SEARCH: LABOR: FILM: TRANS: USE OF FILES:

LOCATION FEE: CATERING:

TRAVEL: AIR FARE: HOTELS: PER DIEM:

TRANSPORTATION: CABS: RENTAL: OTHER:

D SET: DESIGN: LABOR: MATERIALS: STRIKE: O.T.:

E STUDIO MATERIALS: STUDIO RENTAL:

SPECIAL EQUIPMENT: LIGHTING EQUIP.:   GRIP EQUIP.:

F WARDROBE:

G PROPS:

H FILM & PROCESSING: POLAROID: PRINTS: O.T.:

I MESSENGERS: TRUCKING:

J MISC.:   OFFICE EQUIP.:   LD CALLS: GRATUITIES: CATERING:

K INSURANCE:

L MODELS (Studio paid):

PRODUCTION CHARGES:

SUBTOTAL (FEES & CHARGES):

SALES TAX:

CASH ADVANCE:

Balance due upon receipt   BALANCE DUE: _____

Client Signature: _____   Date: _____   Studio Signature: _____
(If Estimate)   (If Invoice)

MODEL fees billed direct

	ADULTS		CHILDREN		EXTRAS	
	NO.	HRS.	NO.	HRS.	NO.	HRS.

Client's usage rights transferred upon full payment of this invoice; subject to all terms and conditions on reverse side.

This form has been approved for use by:
Advertising Photographers of America / Society of Photographer & Artist Representatives
Permission is hereby granted to reproduce this form in whole or in part.

ALL ASSIGNMENTS ARE ACCEPTED SUBJECT TO THE TERMS AND CONDITIONS BELOW, AND THE RIGHTS AND LICENSE GRANTED ARE LIMITED AS FOLLOWS:

A. DEFINITIONS: "Photographer" refers to _____ author of the photographs. "Representative" refers to _____, Photographer's authorized agent. "Client refers to commissioning party, named on the face of this form, and its representatives.

B. QUOTED FEES AND EXPENSES apply to original layout and job description only. Additional compensation must be negotiated with Photographer or Representative for any subsequent changes, additions or variations requested by Client, and confirmed in writing.

C. CANCELLATIONS AND POSTPONEMENTS. (1) In the event that Client does not provide mutually agreed prior notice of cancellation or postponement, Client shall pay 50% of Photographer's fee; except if Client cancels or postpones with less than two business days prior notice, Client shall pay 100% of Photographer's fee. (2) If Client specifies weather conditions for the shoot and postponement is required due to weather, Client shall pay full fee unless postponement is made prior to departure to location, in which event client shall pay 50% of fee. (3) In the event of cancellation or postponement of the booking for any cause other than the Photographer's, Client shall pay all expenses incurred by Photographer as indicated on this form.

D. CLIENT REPRESENTATIVE. Client is responsible for presence of its authorized representative at the shooting to approve Photographer's interpretation of the assignment. If no such representative is present, Client shall accept Photographer's interpretation of the assignment.

E. OVERTIME. (1) Overtime charges shall apply to Photographer on "day rate" only and to all other personnel required to work in excess of eight (8) consecutive hours on any given day. (2) If the shoot lasts beyond the scheduled time, Client shall pay any additional expenses thereby required. (3) Photographer shall provide a schedule of overtime rates at request of Client.

F. RESHOOTS. (1) If film at time of delivery is unusable because of defect, loss or damage   equipment malfunction, processing or other technical error, Photographer shall reshoot without additional fee, and Client shall pay all expenses for the reshoot. (2) If Photographer charges for special contingency insurance (such as PhotoPac) and is paid in full for the shoot, Client shall not be charged for any expenses covered by such insurance. A list of exclusions from such coverage will be provided on request. (3) Client requested changes in completed shoots are subject to additional fee plus all additional expenses.

G. GRANT OF RIGHTS. Grant of any reproduction rights is conditioned on receipt of payment in full. All rights not expressly granted remain the exclusive property of Photographer. Unless otherwise stated on the face of this invoice, duration of license is one year from invoice date, and license is for use in the United States of America only.

H. COPYRIGHT PROTECTION/CREDIT LINE. If Non-Editorial: Client will provide copyright protection by placing proper copyright notice on any use. Proper notice may be either "©Client Name,.Year-date of first publication" (which protects the whole and all of its component parts), or "© _____ 19____" adjacent to or within the photograph(s) (which protects the photographs.)
If Editorial: Credit line in the form "© _____ 19____" in type no smaller than that of related text must appear adjacent to or within the photograph(s) or invoiced fee is tripled.

I. INDEMNITY. Client will indemnify Photographer against any and all claims and expenses, including reasonable counsel fees, arising from its use of Photographer's work.

J. PAYMENT. Invoices are payable upon receipt. 2% per month finance charge is applied on any balances unpaid after 30 days.

K. RETURN OF PHOTOGRAPHS. Client assumes all risk for all original material supplied by Photographer from time of receipt to time of return to Photographer's safekeeping. Client agrees to return all such material by first publication or such other period as is stated on the face of this invoice.

L. LOSS OR DAMAGE. In case of loss or damage, Client agrees that the reasonable value of original transparencies or negatives produced on assignment is $1500.00 each, or triple the total of the invoice, whichever is less.

M. MISCELLANEOUS. Client may not assign or transfer this license. No alterations may be made in the above-stated provisions without the express written consent of Photographer or Representative.

New York Short Form MODEL RELEASES

ADULT RELEASE

     I hereby give _____
permission to use (display, license, sell, publish, etc.) the
photograph(s) made of me on this date for all purposes,
including those of advertising and trade.

_____ _____
  Date   Signature of Adult Subject

Extra Info_____

MINOR RELEASE

     I hereby give _____
permission to use (display, license, sell, publish, etc.) the
photograph(s) made of _____
on this date for all purposes, including those of advertising
and trade.

_____ _____
  Date   Signature of Parent or Guardian

Extra Info_____

N.Y. "LONG FORM" MODEL RELEASE

MINOR RELEASE

      I am the legal guardian of _____
who was born in the year_____, and on his/her behalf I have
granted permission for him/her to be photographed by
_____ on this date.

Minor's Social Security Number:_____

Working Permit #_____Expiration Date:_____

      In consideration of the fees paid or payable on
his/her behalf, I hereby authorize and grant to
_____ the right to use (display,
license use, sell, publish, etc.) the photograph(s) made of
him/her by _____ on this date and to
use his/her name in connection with these photographs for all
purposes and in any publication, form or medium.

      In connection with the foregoing, I hereby release and
hold harmless _____ and his/her
assigns for all liability in the making and use of these
photographs.

_____   _____
Date   Signature of Parent or Guardian

                    _____
                    Signature of Witness

PROPERTY RELEASES

Example #1   PHOTOGRAPHY PERMIT

To whom it may concern:

(Photographer name) is authorized to make photographs at
_____[Describe the premises]_____
during the hours of _____to_____on ___(date or dates)___

_____   _____   _____
Date   Signature   Title

Example #2   PICTURE PERMIT WITH LIMITED RELEASE

___(Photographer name)___ has permission to make photographs
of/on the property at _____
_____[Describe the property]_____
and may use (publish, license, sell, display, etc.) them with
the understanding that additional permission in writing is
required for pictures of this property for purposes of
advertising.

_____   _____   _____
Date   Signature   Title

Example #3   PROPERTY RELEASE   Date:_____

___(Photographer name) and his/her assigns hereby have
permission to make and use photographs of_____
_____[Describe property]_____
made on above date for all purposes, including those of
advertising and trade.

                              _____
                              Signature of owner or
authorized agent

                              _____
                              Title
                              _____
                              Date

Example #4   PROPERTY RELEASE   Date: _____

I hereby release ___(Photographer name)___ and his/her
assigns from any claim of property right (publicity right,
etc.) in images made on the above date of the property
described below:

_____
_____[Describe property]_____

                    _____
                    Signature of owner or authorized agent
          _____   _____
                    Title   Date

APPENDIX C

SOME REFERENCE BOOKS

Books already listed in the text are not included here.

BUSINESS

BUSINESS MANAGEMENT FOR THE PROFESSIONAL PHOTOGRAPHER,
Sy Gutterman. Amphoto division, Watson-Guptill Publications, New York, 1980.

FREELANCE FOREVER: SUCCESSFUL SELF-EMPLOYMENT,
Marietta Whittlesey. Avon Books, New York, 1982.

HOW TO START A PROFESSIONAL PHOTOGRAPHY BUSINESS,
Ted Schwartz. Contemporary Books, Chicago, 1976.

HOW TO START AND MANAGE YOUR OWN BUSINESS,
Gardiner G. Green. McGraw-Hill Book Company, New York, 1980.

PROFESSIONAL BUSINESS PRACTICES IN PHOTOGRAPHY,
American Society of Magazine Photographers, New York, 1982.

THE PHOTOGRAPHER'S BUSINESS HANDBOOK,
John Stockwell and Bert Holtje, editors. McGraw-Hill Book Company, New York, 1980.

ANNUAL PHOTOGRAPHERS' DIRECTORIES

AMERICAN SHOWCASE
American Showcase, Inc., New York.

ART DIRECTOR'S INDEX TO PHOTOGRAPHERS
Rotovision S.A., Geneva; available in U.S.A.

A.S.M.P. ANNUAL OF PROFESSIONAL PHOTOGRAPHY
Annuals Publishing Company, New York.

CORPORATE PHOTOGRAPHY SHOWCASE
American Showcase, Inc., New York.

L.A. WORK BOOK
Alexis Scott, Los Angeles.

MADISON AVENUE HANDBOOK
Peter Glenn Publications, New York.

THE BEST OF PHOTOJOURNALISM
National Press Photographers Association, Durham, NC.

THE CREATIVE BLACK BOOK
Friendly Publications, New York.

OTHER ANNUALS

American Institute of Graphic Arts: GRAPHIC DESIGN USA
Watson-Guptill Publications, New York.

ART DIRECTOR'S ANNUAL
Art Director's Club, Inc., New York.

GRAPHIC ARTISTS GUILD CORPORATE COMMUNICATION AND DESIGN ANNUAL
Annual Publications, New York.

LEGAL AND TAX

FEAR OF FILING
Volunteer Lawyers for the Arts, New York, 1976.

LEGAL GUIDE FOR THE VISUAL ARTIST,
Tad Crawford. Hawthorn Books, New York, 1977.

PHOTOGRAPHY—WHAT'S THE LAW?,
Robert M. Cavallo and Stuart Kahan. Crown Publishers, New York, 1976; revised 1979.

APPENDIX D

PERIODICALS

PHOTO TRADE

INDUSTRIAL PHOTOGRAPHY
475 Park Avenue South, New York, NY 10016

INTERNATIONAL PHOTOGRAPHY
Eastman Kodak Company, 343 State Street, Rochester, NY 14650

NEWS PHOTOGRAPHER
National Press Photographers Association publication
Box 1146, Durham, NC 27702

PHOTO DISTRICT NEWS
167 Third Avenue, New York, NY 10003

PHOTOMETHODS
1 Park Avenue, New York, NY 10016

THE PROFESSIONAL PHOTOGRAPHER
Professional Photographers of America journal
1090 Executive Way, Des Plaines, IL 60018

THE RANGEFINDER
1312 Lincoln Boulevard, Santa Monica, CA 90406

STUDIO LIGHT
Eastman Kodak Company, 343 State Street, Rochester, NY 14650

STUDIO PHOTOGRAPHY
250 Fulton Avenue, Hempstead, NY 11550

TECHNICAL PHOTOGRAPHY
250 Fulton Avenue, Hempstead, NY 11550

GENERAL

AMERICAN PHOTOGRAPHER
1515 Broadway, New York, NY 10036

APERTURE
Elm Street, Millerton, NY 12546
DARKROOM PHOTOGRAPHY
609 Mission Street, San Francisco, CA 94105
MODERN PHOTOGRAPHY
825 Seventh Avenue, New York, NY 10019
PETERSEN'S PHOTOGRAPHIC MAGAZINE
8490 Sunset Boulevard, Los Angeles, CA 90010
PHOTO
65 Champs-Elysées, Paris 75008, France
POPULAR PHOTOGRAPHY
1 Park Avenue, New York, NY 10016

GRAPHIC DESIGN

ART DIRECTION
19 West 44th Street, New York, NY 10036
CA—COMMUNICATION ARTS
P.O. Box 10300, Palo Alto, CA 94303
PRINT
355 Lexington Avenue, New York, NY 10016
(also publishes "Print's Regional Design Annual").

APPENDIX E

PROFESSIONAL ORGANIZATIONS

Membership in a professional organization has many advantages. You not only stay on top of the technical, legal, and social aspects of your business, but you also get to meet the competition. Information exchanged by members about clients, prices, marketing, equipment sources, and the work in general can be invaluable, especially to the professional who is just beginning a career.

Most of the addresses and telephone numbers listed here are for the groups' national headquarters. In many cases there are local chapters of these organizations, but you can write the national offices for information.

ADVERTISING PHOTOGRAPHERS OF AMERICA (A.P.A.)
118 East 25th Street, New York, NY 10010. (212) 254-5500.
For photographers working primarily in advertising in large-to-medium markets.

AMERICAN SOCIETY OF MAGAZINE PHOTOGRAPHERS (A.S.M.P.)
205 Lexington Avenue, New York, NY 10016. (212) 889-9144.
Large organization of photographers working in editorial, advertising, corporate, and related fields.

AMERICAN SOCIETY OF PICTURE PROFESSIONALS (A.S.P.P.)
Box 5283, Grand Central Station, New York, NY 10017.
Photographers, picture researchers, stock photo agencies, and others involved in production and use of editorial photography.

BIOLOGICAL PHOTOGRAPHIC ASSOCIATION
6650 Northwest Highway, Chicago, IL 60631.
Biomedical photographers and technicians.

EVIDENCE PHOTOGRAPHERS INTERNATIONAL COUNCIL
601 Brookview Court, Oxford, OH 45056. (513) 523-8092.
Law enforcement and legal photographers.

INTERNATIONAL ALLIANCE OF THEATRICAL AND STAGE
EMPLOYEES (IATSE)
Local 644, 250 West 57th Street, New York, NY 10019. (212) 247-3860.
Local 659, 7715 Sunset Blvd., Hollywood, CA 90046. (213) 876-0160. Local
666, 327 South LaSalle Street, Chicago, IL 60604. (312) 341-0966. Union
photographers on motion picture and TV productions.

NATIONAL PRESS PHOTOGRAPHERS ASSOCIATION (N.P.P.A.)
Box 1146, Durham, NC 27702. (919) 489-3700.
Photojournalists.

PROFESSIONAL PHOTOGRAPHERS OF AMERICA (P.P. of A.)
1090 Executive Way, Des Plaines, IL 60018. (312) 299-8161.
Portrait, wedding, industrial, forensic, and commercial photographers.

SOCIETY OF PHOTOGRAPHERS AND ARTISTS REPRESENTATIVES
(SPAR)
Box 845, F.D.R. Station, New York, NY 10022. (212) 832-3213.
The national organization of reps.

APPENDIX F

COPYRIGHT AND PRACTICE OF THE TRADE

Edith and Phillip Leonian   ©Edith and Phillip Leonian

The stated intent of Congress in enacting the copyright law which took effect January 1st, 1978, was to foster "original works of authorship" and "new forms of creative expression" by vesting control of these works in the hands of their creators.

While there are basic conceptual changes in the new law, it was written with an eye to the "practice of the trade" which developed under the old law, so as far as the course of ordinary business is concerned, the effective changes have proved to be more of detail than substance.

Those few problems which have arisen have been due largely to lack of information on the part of the artists and their clients, or to misunderstandings, by both lawyers and laymen, as to how the new law does affect business practice.

This article is intended as a simplified look at those areas of the Copyright Act of 1976 (Public Law 94-553) which have proved to be of most concern to photographers, illustrators and their clients in the law's first year.

A caveat: while the law itself is straightforward and easy to understand, copyright disputes can become extremely complex. Answers are dependent on the specifics of each particular case. An experienced copyright attorney should be consulted on any problems, as most general attorneys lack the background to fully appreciate its ramifications.

First Ownership. Under the old law, work specially commissioned was considered "work made for hire," so the client owned the copyright in absence of agreement to the contrary. In practice, most photographers and illustrators limited the client's copyright by specifying permitted use in advertising, or one time reproduction in editorial work.

Under the new law, the photographers, illustrator or other author of an original work owns the copyright unless he signs an agreement to the contrary.

166

In other words, photographers and illustrators no longer have to negotiate for copyright. They own it from the instant of creation—"When it is fixed in a copy for the first time"—that is, the instant the film is exposed.

Transfer of Rights. The most single visible change in business practice caused by the new law is that any reproduction or derivative rights to a work must be transferred in writing.[1] In addition this transfer of rights, or license, must be signed by the creator or his or her authorized agent.

Copyright can no longer be legally transferred by verbal agreement. The new law supercedes common law copyright, and pre-empts any state law which deals with copyright matters.

Adding to the importance of the written transfer is the fact that under the new law, copyright is infinitely divisible—not one right, but a bundle of little rights which may be sold or assigned by the first owner (the photographer, illustrator, or other author).

The concept is familiar in editorial work, but in advertising and other commercial work neither user nor supplier has been accustomed to spelling out what is being bought and what is being sold up front. Wording was loose, tacit understanding common. It worked, after a fashion. But it was also the cause of ninety percent of the misunderstandings between users of art and photography and their creative resources.

Now, under the new law, in order for buyers of art to be sure they have the rights they need in an assignment, is is important for them to tell the photographer or other author what they are in advance, so that the author can grant those rights.

Since art directors or other buyers don't always know all the uses which will be made of a photograph in advance, the practice has continued to be for clients to buy only those rights they know they'll need. Then they either negotiate for additional rights as the need arises, or pre-negotiate fees so that they would know in advance the cost of any additional use.

Since abiding by these written agreements is now a matter of law rather than one of ethics, the effect thus far has been to reduce the number of after-the-fact disputes.

Therefore, since divisibility of rights has extensively enhanced the earning potential of a transparency or other artwork, "all rights" transactions, with their concomitantly higher fees, have been relatively rare.

Copyright Notice. Under the old law, if copyright notice failed to appear on a published work, even by accident, that work lost its copyright protection and entered the public domain.

The new law continues to call for notice on copies distributed to the public, but absence of notice, or error in notice, will not immediately result in loss of copyright.

Because of the provisions made for correction (§405 of the law), the need for notice has been played down and taken a bit too lightly in certain cases in the law's first year, which may yet result in a large body of work entering the public domain unless corrective steps are taken.

I. Improper Notice. Proper notice contains three elements:
A. The letter c in a circle—©; the word "copyright" or the abbreviation "copr";

B. The year of the first publication of the work (or, in the case of previously unpublished work created prior to Jan. 1, 1978, the year1978); C. The name of the copyright owner. If all three elements are not present, copyright protection does not ensue, and a correction must be filed. The most common error in notice has been the omission of the year date in credit lines for individual photographs.

II. Individual Notice for Advertisements. Advertisements are specifically mentioned only one time in the entire copyright law—and that mention is not only negative but parenthetical. §404 (1) provides that copyright notice for a "collective work" (such as a magazine, newspaper, or other periodical) does not protect advertisements inserted in that publication.

In other words, if an advertisement does not carry a copyright notice of its own, and subsequent corrective steps are not taken, it will enter the public domain. This means that it, or any of its elements, may be reproduced at will by anyone, for any purpose, whatever the wishes of the advertiser whose property the ad would otherwise be.

Leafing through the pages of any magazine during the past year or so, one will find many too many ads without copyright notice. As very few advertisers wish to dedicate these expensive pages to the good of the public, absence of notice can only result from ignorance or poor legal advice.

For this reason photographers and illustrators have been advised by their professional associations to include as a standard condition of sale on any of their licenses (invoices) that the user of the work shall provide copyright protection for it. This makes it possible for them to take advantage of corrective registration if necessary.

Even if a correction is filed, omission of notice can still provide a defense of "innocent infringement." And advertisers would keep in mind that Europeans, accustomed to American requirements for notice, routinely assume that any work published in the U.S.A. without a notice is in the public domain, and feel they can reproduce it at will.

An object Lesson: Each advertisement in the PAPA Directory carries individual copyright notice for the photographer placing the ad.

This does protect the advertisement as a whole, and its copyrightable elements, under the law.

This does not mean that the photographer necessarily owns all of the rights in each of the images he displays. The copyright in an original work like a photograph is separate or distinct from the copyright of a large work in which it is incorporated.

This sounds confusing, and often is. The best way to clarify ownership of individual images, ease registration and prevent disputes in such cases is for each individual illustration to carry separate notice.

III. Copyright Notice for the Photograph or Illustration. Photographers and illustrators have also been advised by their professional societies to make individual and adjacent copyright notice a standard condition of sale. Then, if the notice is "left off" an ad (where trade practice has not been to carry photographer credits), the Copyright Office can treat it as an error that is correctable by registration. Registration by the photographer saves the copyright of the photograph.

If the advertiser wishes to correct a notice deficiency, then he, she, or it must use the alternate methods mentioned in §405 of the law.

In periodicals and other "collective works," the copyright notice of the magazine itself prevents the editorial contents from falling into the public domain. If the photographer's copyright notice appears adjacent to his or her work, however, she or he will enjoy the advantages of bulk registration (the best protection of a year's work for a single $10 fee) and protection against claims of innocent infringement.

Since copyright notice also serves as a credit line, it imposes no hardship on magazines where such credit has long been customary. Adjacent copyright notice in magazines is taking the place of the simple credit line as a hallmark of those photographers and other authors who value their work. Many go so far as to impose penalites of two or three times invoiced fees if specified adjacent notice is omitted editorially.

IV. Another New Notice Requirement: Foreign Publication. American work published abroad must be protected by copyright notice in its foreign publication, or its American copyright protection is abrogated. In other words, if a photograph or other work appears in another country without notice, it enters the public domain here. This change was made to conform to Universal Copyright Convention requirements.

Elements of a Proper Copyright License. The photographer, illustrator or other author and the client should agree up front on the rights being purchased, the fees and negotiable terms and conditions. It is recommended that the author list this information on an unsigned assignment confirmation form, with a copy to the client. Then, upon delivery, the photographer's invoice will serve as transfer of stated reproduction rights, or the copyright license. This should include:

I. Description of the photograph, illustration or other work being licensed;

II. Rights being granted;

III. Fees and expenses;

IV. Standard duration of license is now generally one year from invoice date;

V. As a condition of sale: that the client copyright his product (magazine, ad, slide, film, brochure, billboard, package, etc.);

VI. As a condition of sale: that the photographer, illustrator or other author receive adjacent copyright notice in legal form;

VII. Under 202 of the new law, purchase of reproduction rights is separate from purchase of the object (original transparency or other artwork), so terms and conditions for return of originals should be included, unless originals are separately purchased. (A bonus for buyers is that, at least in New York State, no sales tax is due if originals are returned undamaged and unchanged—a saving of 8% of the total of the invoice in New York);

VIII. Any other terms and conditions (payment terms, finance charges, model release requirements, etc.);

IX. Any restrictions important to the photographer or other author— for instance, "no cropping" for Henri Cartier-Bresson (to be agreed upon up front);

X. Last, but far from least, because without it the license is not sufficient under the new law: THE SIGNATURE OF THE

PHOTOGRAPHER/ILLUSTRATOR/AUTHOR OR HIS OR HER AU-
THORIZED AGENT.

Remember that the prime purpose of a properly drawn license with
its clarity of terms is to facilitate business, prevent disputes and stay out
of court.

Duration of Copyright. Under the new law, the creator's term of
copyright on work created after Jan. 1, 1978, is his or her life plus fifty
years. Work created before Jan. 1, 1978, but neither published nor in the
public domain prior to that date, is protected for the creator's life plus
fifty years.

Anonymous works, pseudonymous works or works made for hire
receive copyright for a term of seventy-five years from the year of first
publication, or one hundrd years from year of creation, whichever ex-
pires first.

Which brings up a side issue.

Work Made for Hire. "Work made for hire" is the exception to the
new law's rule that copyright vests in the creator. In 101 of the law, there
are two definitions of "work made for hire" which allow an employer
author status.

"(1) a work prepared by an employee within the scope of his or her
employment; or

"(2) a work specially ordered or commissioned for use as a contri-
bution to a collective work...if the parties expressly agree in a written
instrument signed by them that work shall be considered a 'work made
for hire.' "

"Collective work" as referred to in the law has a very specific
meaning: "A collective work is a special kind of compilation; it must
include a number of contributions, each of which must constitute 'separate and independent work in themselves,' and these individual parts
must be assembled into a 'collective' as distinguished from a 'unitary'
whole, thus leaving integrated works...outside the definition."[2]

Therefore, according to Barbara Ringer,[3] Register of Copyrights in
the United States, very few advertisements involving individual contractors can qualify as "work made for hire." In fact it would be easier to list
who is eligible to ask for it than who is not.

Magazines, newspapers, and other periodicals are eligible to ask
for "work for hire," but only if the photographer or other author agrees to
it in advance, in writing, in an instrument signed by both parties.

There is only one difference aside from the duration of copyright
between a "work made for hire" and "all rights." On any license of
copyright, the author has the right to terminate the grant of rights after
thirty-five years. In a "work for hire," the author does not have that right.

This is rather remote, and the phrase "work made for hire" would
be copyright curiosa if it had not been incorporated into some pre-
employment contracts a few magazines sent to their contributors last
year.

Editors for the most part found little need for the contracts once
they found out what they meant. While some continue to offer them for
signature, in most cases refusal to sign has had no effect on whether or
not an author, photographer or illustrator received an assignment.

There are two reasons for this. Historically magazine publishers have bargained for the lowest possible rates in return for acquiring very limited rights, commonly one time reproduction rights. They are still unwilling to pay the much higher fees that go along with the purchase of extensive, or "all," rights.

Second, serious legal questions have been raised concerning the validity of "blanket" pre-employment contracts for indepenent contractors, both on the grounds of the intent of Congress, and, interestingly, on anti-trust grounds.

To Know More. Space does not permit a full discussion of the copyright laws here. The Copyright Office has available its excellent A General Guide to the Copyright Act of 1976 for the price of a stamp or phone call. You can also get copies of the law, as many of the commentaries as you can stomach, registration forms and instructions, and additional information on the formalities.

The address is: The Copyright Office
              Library of Congress
              Washington, DC 20559

The telephone number is 202/287-8700. They have added a 24 hour "hot line" to order registration forms: 202/287-9100.

The Copyright Office under Barbara Ringer[3] has the reputation of being efficient and responsive—a rarity among federal bureaucracies. If you call, you'll find the phone answered by an informed and helpful person who can either provide the information you seek or direct you to someone who can.

---

[1]The one exception is that work submitted to a periodical (magazine, or newspaper) may be used in that publication without written license—but also without alteration, abridgement, cropping, etc.

[2]Marlene D. Morrisey, Special Assistant to the Register of Copyrights, in a 3M Co. supplement to Business Week.

[3]Barbara Ringer left the Copyright Office to write the definitive book on the new copyright law, and to practice law privately. The new Register is David Ladd.

APPENDIX G

Job Jacket

JOB NO. _____   DATE _____

PURCHASE ORDER NO. _____   INVOICE NO. _____

CLIENT	PHOTOGRAPHER	FEE
AGENCY	JOB DESCRIPTION	
ART DIRECTOR		
PRODUCTS		

GENERAL EXPENSES

STYLIST	
PROPS	
CASTING	
LOCATION	
MODELS	
TRANSPORTATION	
MESSENGER	
ASSISTANT	
MISCELLANEOUS	

FILM, PROCESSING & PRINT EXPENSES

FILM & PROCESSING	
PRINTS	

DATE CLIENT BILLED	TOTAL _____
DATE BILL PAID	SALES TAX _____
	TOTAL DUE _____

APPENDIX H

Shot Record

HOLDER NUMBER	SHOT DESCRIPTION	LIGHTS	F STOP	LENS	FORMAT EMULS.	FILTER	DEV.	NOTES

JOB NUMBER: DATE: JOB DESCRIPTION:

INDEX

A

Ability to Deliver Product, 8
Accessories, 67, 73
Advertising, 17, 18, 20, 22, 24, 55,
    121, 130
  agencies, 19, 21, 23, 25, 32, 34,
    35–38, 48, 52, 91
  annuals, 88
  corporate in-house agency,
    48–49
  directories, 83–84, 122
  magazine, 39
  portfolio for, 100–101
  rates for, 117, 149
  working in, 13, 14, 15
Agent ("Rep"), 12, 103–104,
    129–31
Annual Reports, 51–52
Answering Services, 140–41
Architectural Photography, 16,
    20, 31, 38, 39, 44
  rates for, 117
Art and Design Schools, 58–59
Art Director, 113
  of advertising agency, 37–38,
    48, 101, 122

of audiovisual firm, 47
of design studio, 39
Art-Supply Store, 75
Assisting a Photographer, 55,
    60–66, 82
Audiovisual Production House,
    20, 21, 23, 35, 45–47, 48
  directories, 84–85
  portfolio for, 101

B

Bags, 68, 73
Bank Account (Business), 137
Baraban, Joe, 54–55
Baughman, Ross, 41–42, 77–78
Beauty Photography, 15, 20, 31,
    35, 38, 39, 44, 48
Billing for Services (Getting
    Paid), 9, 70, 79, 80, 114,
    116–31, 132
  costing factors, 119–21
  experience counts, 116–17
  getting price in writing, 123,
    125–26

R

S

T